The Chronicle of Jocelin

of Brakelond

A Picture of Monastic Life in the Days of

Abbot Samson

Jocelin de Brakelond

Editor:

Sir Ernest Clarke

Alpha Editions

This edition published in 2021

ISBN : 9789355348630

Design and Setting By
Alpha Editions
www.alphaedis.com
Email – info@alphaedis.com

PREFACE

Samson and his Arch-Eulogist.—Abbot Samson of St. Edmundsbury and his biographer, Jocelin of Brakelond, undoubtedly owe such immortality as they possess to their introduction to the world at large by Thomas Carlyle. Learned historians and commentators of the past had made use of the dry facts of the Chronicle for their disquisitions and treatises; but none had recognized the human interest of Jocelin's narrative until the Sage of Chelsea seized upon it as evidence of that theory of Hero Worship on which he loved to insist.

The whole of the seventeen chapters of Book II. of "Past and Present," published in 1843, are devoted to a study of Abbot Samson, and the lessons which Carlyle thought "our own poor century" could learn from him.

From that day to this, Samson has been more or less a household word; and, as John Richard Green says in his "Stray Studies" (1876), "In the wandering gossipy pages of Jocelin of Brakelond the life of the twelfth century, so far as it could penetrate abbey walls, still glows distinct for us round the figure of the shrewd, practical, kindly, imperious abbot who looks out, a little travestied perhaps, from the pages of Mr. Carlyle."

The Chronicle.—Mr. Green further says:—"By a rare accident the figure of the silent, industrious Norfolk monk, who at the close of Henry the Second's reign suddenly found himself ruler of the wealthiest, if not the greatest, of English abbeys, starts out distinct from the dim canvas of the annals of his house. Annals indeed in any strict sense St. Edmund's has none; no national chronicle was ever penned in its scriptorium such as that which flings lustre round its rival, St. Albans; nor is even a record of its purely monastic life preserved such as that which gives a local and ecclesiastical interest to its rival of Glastonbury. One book alone the abbey has given us, but that one book is worth a thousand chronicles."

The original manuscript of the Chronicle occupies 43 folios (121-163) of a thick quarto volume on vellum once in the library of Bury Abbey, afterwards in the hands of the family of Bacon of Redgrave, then belonging to Bishop Stillingfleet of Worcester, and now preserved in the British Museum amongst the Harleian Manuscripts. The contents of this *Liber Albus* (Harl. MS. 1005) are very varied; and a complete list of the 144 items in it which relate to the Abbey will be found on pp. 122-4 of the 1821 Edition of the *Monasticon*. (Another copy of the Chronicle was in the Cottonian MS. Vitellius DXV., burnt in the fire of 1731.) Three facsimiles of portions of the

MS. are given in the Camden Society's Edition of the Latin text (to be presently referred to), and the writing is there ascribed to the end of the 13th or beginning of the 14th century.

Previous Editions of the Chronicle.—In the year 1840, John Gage Rokewode, F.R.S. (1786-1842), Director of the Society of Antiquaries, brought out for the Camden Society a thin quarto book in the familiar green cover, which he entitled "Chronica Jocelini de Brakelonda de rebus gestis Samsonis Abbatis Monasterii Sancti Edmundi." It was this book that attracted the attention of Carlyle, with the results already stated. Rokewode was a scion of the distinguished family of Gage of Hengrave, near Bury, and took the additional name of Rokewode on inheriting in 1838 the estates of the Rookwood family. He was a very learned genealogist, and the author of a History of Hengrave and of the Hundred of Thingoe. His observations on Suffolk families and topography are therefore to be relied upon, though subsequent investigation has corrected some of his notes on historical matters.

Rokewode's text was in the original Latin; but to meet the popular demand for the Chronicle caused by Carlyle's published appreciation of it in "Past and Present" (1843), a translation into English was made by Thomas Edlyne Tomlins (1804-1872), and was published in 1844 by Whitaker & Co. in the "Popular Library of Modern Authors," under the title of "Monastic and Social Life in the Twelfth Century."

Mr. T. E. Tomlins was a nephew of the better known Sir Thomas Edlyne Tomlins (1762-1841), assistant counsel to the Treasury, who wrote "The Law of Wills" and other well-known text-books. The younger Thomas was an attorney, and also wrote on legal subjects. Tomlins' translation of Jocelin was issued in the somewhat forbidding form of a tall paper-covered book of 64 pages of double columns of small type, without any break from start to finish: the few notes at the end being mostly on legal points, and none of them of great merit.

It does not appear that Mr. Tomlins had any special knowledge of his subject; and, as a consequence, his translation contained a quantity of errors, both of omission and commission. His book has been used as the ground-work for the present edition, but the alterations made in the text have been so numerous and important as to be practically equivalent to a new translation altogether. The three Appendices (pages 215-278) are wholly new.

The task of rendering the Latin text into satisfactory and accurate English has been made easier by the publication in 1890-6 of Mr. Thomas Arnold's three volumes of "Memorials of St. Edmund's Abbey" (No. 96 of the Rolls Series). "Tom" Arnold (1823-1900) was the second son of Arnold of Rugby and the younger brother of Matthew Arnold; and he undertook a quantity of work for the Rolls Series, not all of which he was able to carry through with the completeness that he desired. Especially with regard to the Annals of St. Edmundsbury there was a quantity of material that he could not deal with in the leisure at his command. But so far as concerns the Chronicle of Jocelin (which occupies 228 pages of his Volume I.), his edition of the original Latin text was carefully revised and annotated.

The Chronicler.—Of Jocelin of Brakelond very little is certainly known beyond what he himself tells us in the Chronicle. There are two streets in Bury St. Edmunds known as the Long and Short Brackland or Braklond, and probably Jocelin took his name from his place of birth. In the text of the Chronicle, however, and in other 13th century documents in which his name is recorded, he appears simply as Jocelin. He tells us he took the habit in 1173, "the year when the Flemings were taken captive without the town" (page 1); and that he then came under the care of Samson, at that time master of the novices, who told him some of his own experiences by way of warning against interference with the constituted authorities (6).

At the time of Samson's election as Abbot, in 1182, Jocelin was prior's chaplain, but within four months he was made abbot's chaplain, "noting many things and committing them to memory" (39): for which all students of English history are eternally grateful to him. In his capacity as Samson's chaplain, Jocelin was "constantly with him by day and night for six years, and had the opportunity of becoming fully conversant with the worthiness of his life and the wisdom of his rule" (56).

Jocelin evidently starts at first with an admiration for Samson's vigorous and independent régime (see especially pages 52-3); but later on his faith in his master seems to have been a little shaken, and Samson's action in practically "jockeying" his favourite Herbert into the office of prior takes Jocelin's breath away. The eventful meeting of the chapter over, he sits down stupefied in the porch of the guest chamber (he being then hospitarius), and reflects on the situation (198). He cannot approve, moreover, Samson's action with regard to John Ruffus and Adam the Infirmarer, where he more than hints at the Abbot's acceptance of a bribe (200). The banking up by Samson of the fishpond at Babwell, thus flooding the pastures and gardens of others, he describes as "another stain of evil doing" (201): the Abbot's passionate retort that "his fish pond was not to be spoilt on account of our meadows," obviously offending Jocelin's sense of the proprieties. He demurs, moreover, to the willingness of certain of the monks to strip even the shrine of St. Edmund himself to obtain an exemption of the Abbey from episcopal visitation, pointing out that there might come a time when the convent might need the control of a bishop, archbishop, or legate, over a tyrannous or spendthrift abbot (7).

It is perhaps for these reasons that we find Jocelin, at a date after Samson's death, on the side of the party of caution and moderation in the disputes over the election of a new abbot. The author, whoever he was, of the interpolated narrative in the Chronicle relating to Henry of Essex (101 *et seq.*) refers to "Master Jocelin our almoner, a man of exalted piety, powerful in word and in deed"; and there can hardly be any doubt that this was our Jocelin. In the highly complicated story (printed in Mr. Arnold's second volume) of the preliminaries to the final approval by King John of Samson's successor, Abbot Hugh II., Jocelin the almoner took the side of Robert of Gravelee, the sacrist, who advocated the adoption of the plan followed when the previous vacancy occurred, of submitting to the king names from whom he could make a selection (as indeed John had asked might be done by letter dated 25 July, 1213), instead of asking him, as they did, to confirm an election already made. Jocelin, in a speech delivered in the chapter-house, seems indeed to have been the first to start the view that the convent had made a mistake, and that it ought to put itself right with the king. He again insisted on this at a second debate in December, 1213, and took a prominent part in the subsequent discussions, his name being recorded in the division list of June, 1214, when 30 voted on his side, and 32 for adherence to the claims of the Abbey.

The three delegates, the Abbot of Wardon, the Prior of Dunstable, and the Dean of Salisbury, who had been appointed by the Pope on May 18, 1214, to inquire into the Bury election, held the last but one of their numerous sittings on February 12, 1215, at which Jocelin was present. At last the delegates announced on March 10 their judgment confirming the election, which, with considerable trouble, they persuaded the sacrist and his party to accept, and to exchange with the new abbot the kiss of peace.

When, on April 24, 1215, the abbot elect, unsuccessful in obtaining John's favour, and refusing to bribe the king, though advised to do so by the courtiers, appointed certain officials to the custody of Abbey manors, he took the advice, amongst other high officers, of Jocelin the almoner; and this is the last we hear of our Chronicler.

Jocelin himself mentions (23) that he had written a book on the many signs and wonders in connection with the martyrdom by the Jews of the boy Robert, who was buried in the Abbey Church; but this work is not known to be extant. The inaccurate Bale also ascribes to him the authorship of the tract *Super Electione Hugonis* (also in the Liber Albus), from which the above facts as to Jocelin's later life have been gleaned. But there is no authority for this; and, as Mr. Arnold points out (i. lix.), the style of that work is different from the Chronicle.

Whatever criticisms one might be tempted to pass on Carlyle's appreciation of Samson, there need be no dissentient voice to his summing up of Jocelin's character:—

An ingenious and ingenuous, a cheery-hearted, innocent, yet withal shrewd, noticing, quick-witted man; and from under his monk's cowl has looked out on the narrow section of the world in a really human manner.... The man is of patient, peaceable, loving, clear-smiling nature; open for this or that.... Also he has a pleasant wit, and loves a timely joke, though in mild, subdued manner. A learned, grown man, yet with the heart as of a good child.

The Central Figure of the Chronicle.—Whatever his other merits, Jocelin's strong point was certainly not chronological sequence. With the assistance of the Table of Dates printed on pages 261-267, the reader will, it is hoped, get some useful sort of idea of the busy life of Abbot Samson, both within and without the walls of the monastery, whilst it was under his vigorous rule; and as to his personal characteristics, virtues and foibles, they are writ large in almost every chapter of the Chronicle.

He was obviously of humble origin, and his dialect was that of his native county of Norfolk (62). He seems to have lost his father early, for we read of his conferring, soon after he became Abbot, a benefice upon the son of a man of lowly station who had been kind to him in his youth and looked after his interests (66). As a child of nine, he had been taken by his mother to a pilgrimage to St. Edmund, after a dream which presaged his future service under that saint (56). When he was a poor clerk, William, the schoolmaster of Diss, had given him free admission to his school: a favour which he requited by giving Walter, son of William, the living of Chevington (67). Similarly, he helped those of his kinsmen who had recognized him when he was a poor clerk, provided they were worthy; but with those who had then held aloof from him he wished to have no dealings (66).

At some early date Samson went to Paris to study, a friend who then supported him there by the proceeds of the sale of holy water receiving afterwards a benefice from him (66). Just as he did not forget the friends who had helped him in his early struggles so he remembered past kindnesses shown to him when he was a poor monk and out of favour with the authorities. When Hugh, his predecessor, clapped him into irons, Hugh's cupbearer Elias brought him some wine to quench his prison thirst (67); and when he needed a night's lodging on his return from Durham on the business of the Abbey, a resident at Risby gave him the shelter which a neighbour refused (68). Neither favour was forgotten when Elias and William of Risby came before him as landlord.

By 1160 Samson was back from abroad as master of the schools at Bury, though he did not become a professed monk till 1166. Meanwhile he had been sent on an errand to Rome, with reference to the church at Woolpit, in which his native wit showed itself (73, 74). He seems to have been successful in his mission, getting from Pope Alexander III. a reversion for the monastery of the Woolpit living; but, perhaps because he returned too late to prevent Geoffrey Ridel being appointed by the king (74), Abbot Hugh banished him, on his return, to Castle Acre. Here he remained in exile a long time (74), and he was sent there again after he had become a cloister monk, and had spoken up "for the good of our Church" in opposition to the Abbot (6).

Samson in Subordinate Offices.—Much as Hugh disliked Samson, he seems to have been a little afraid of him; and, to reconcile matters, he made Samson subsacrist. "Often accused," says Jocelin, "he was transferred from one office to another, being successively guest master, pittance master, third prior, and again subsacrist" (9). But he could not be induced to fawn on and flatter the Abbot, as other officials did; and Hugh declared that "he had never seen a man whom he could not bend to his will, except Samson the subsacrist" (10).

When at length Hugh's trying dispensation came to an end, through his horse accident at Canterbury in 1180, Samson was, as subsacrist, busy with new building operations for the Church (14). His superior officer, the bibulous William Wiardel, the sacrist, was jealous of him, and persuaded the wardens of the Abbey to stop any further expense for works during the vacancy (15). But Samson knew some things to William's financial and moral discredit, on which he was later able to base the sacrist's dismissal from office (46-7).

The gossip amongst the monks as to which of the brethren should fill Hugh's place is admirably told by Jocelin (Chap. ii.). Whilst the rest were babbling at blood-letting season, Samson the subsacrist sat smiling but saying nothing (21). The receipt of Henry II.'s order or permission to make choice of a new Abbot put the monastery in a flutter; and the selection of the deputation to wait upon the King, and their interview with their liege lord, is most naïvely described in chapter iii. The secret ballot at Bury for three names was a surprise to the higher officials (31), and they did what they could to diminish Samson's chances. But after some fencing the Bishop of Winchester asked the deputation point blank whom they wanted, and the answer was—Samson: "no one gainsaying this" (34).

Samson as Abbot.—And so the once oppressed and obscure monk returned to Bury the absolute ruler of the foundation, with the king's remark in his ears when he noted, with apparent admiration at Bishop's Waltham, how Samson comported himself in the royal presence: "By the eyes of God, this Abbot elect thinks himself worthy to govern an abbey!" (35). So indeed he did, setting to work at once after his ceremonial installation (37) to institute reforms of all sorts. As Carlyle says, and his words must suffice in this place:—

How Abbot Samson, giving his new subjects seriatim the kiss of fatherhood in the St. Edmundsbury chapter-house, proceeded with cautious energy to set about reforming their disjointed, distracted way of life; how he managed with his Fifty rough Milites (Feudal Knights), with his lazy farmers, remiss refractory monks, with Pope's Legates, Viscounts, Bishops, Kings; how on all sides he laid about him like a man, and putting consequence on premiss, and everywhere the saddle on the right horse, struggled incessantly to educe organic method out of lazily fermenting wreck,—the careful reader will discern, not without true interest, in these pages of Jocelin Boswell.

To tell the story of all this would be to paraphrase the Chronicle; and the reader is therefore referred to the List of Contents for instances of the Abbot's capacity and resourcefulness in dealing with the complicated interests under his control.

But there is one aspect of his busy life to which allusion may perhaps here be made, as showing the influence and importance of the Abbot of St. Edmundsbury outside the monastery walls.

Relations with Church and State.—Samson's abbacy extended over the pontificates of five Popes and the reigns of three Kings, by all of whom his strength of character and wisdom of counsel seem to have been appreciated. Pope Lucius III., who had succeeded, in 1181, Alexander III., to whom Samson had twenty years before paid a visit on behalf of the Abbey (72), appointed the new abbot a judge in the ecclesiastical courts within seven months of his election (51). Urban III. granted Samson in 1187-8, the privilege of giving the episcopal benediction (84) and other concessions. Celestine III. placed him in 1197 on the commission for restoring the expelled monks at Coventry (142); and Innocent III. granted on December 1, 1198, without hesitation, on Samson's application, an exemption of Bury Abbey from episcopal visitation even by a legate unless he were a legate *a latere* (124).

King Henry II., who had apparently formed a favourable opinion of Samson from his demeanour on his election (35), practically decided in his favour on February 11, 1187, in his dispute with Archbishop Hubert concerning his abbatial jurisdiction over Monk's Eleigh, where a case of homicide had occurred (78). In the same year, the king at Clarendon favourably considered Samson's petition with reference to the immunity of Bury Abbey from certain taxes (96). Having taken the Cross on January 21, 1188, Henry II. came to Bury within a month to pay a pilgrimage to St.

Edmund, when Samson endeavoured, without success, to obtain the king's permission to do likewise (81).

In the next year Henry died at Chinon (July 6, 1189), and Samson had to deal with a new sovereign: at whose coronation on September 3, 1189, he was present. One of Richard's earliest acts was the sale of offices, crown rights, crown property, and royal favours to fill his military chest; saying indeed that he would sell London if he could find a purchaser. Amongst the bargains of this sort was the sale to Samson of the manor of Mildenhall for 1,000 marks, after the astute abbot had offered him half that amount (70). The queen-mother was entitled by custom of the realm to 100 marks as a perquisite in connection with this transaction, and took in lieu thereof a gold cup which had been given to the abbey by Henry II. This same cup came back to Bury in exchange for 100 marks (71), when the 70,000 marks required to ransom King Richard was being raised in England (147).

When the news of Richard's capture reached England, Samson rose in his place in the King's Council to express his readiness to seek the king in Germany, either in disguise or any other way: "by reason whereof," says Jocelin, "he obtained great approbation" (81). Later on he did go to Germany, "and visited the king with many gifts" (82).

Towards the end of Richard's reign, in 1198, Samson tried to avoid sending four of his knights to Normandy, in obedience to the King's orders, and went to see him, with the result that Richard accepted four mercenaries, and afterwards a hundred pounds to discharge the obligation (128-30). He brought back with him on this occasion for the adornment of the abbey church a golden cross and a valuable copy of the Gospels (130); and Jocelin records that so often as he returned from beyond sea on his numerous visits abroad, he brought back with him some offering for the church (131), besides making gifts to it on other occasions.

In 1198 a serious quarrel took place between Richard and Samson over the wardship of Nesta of Cockfield, the daughter of a family whose tenure of lands from the Abbey is recorded with wearisome iteration in the Chronicle. Samson would not give way, despite the threats of the King, which he "very wisely passed over without notice," and in the end Richard yielded with a good grace, asking the abbot if he would send him some of his dogs. The abbot of course complied, and added some horses and other valuable gifts, in exchange for which Richard sent him a ring given to him by the new Pope, Innocent III. (147-9).

Just as Samson had "obtained the favour and grace of King Richard by gifts and money, so that he had good reason to believe that he could succeed in all his undertakings, the King died, and the abbot lost all his labour and outlay" (178). It became therefore necessary to propitiate Richard's successor. King John made an early pilgrimage to St. Edmund, but left in bad odour with the monastery, which had spent much money on his entertainment, but had only received in return thirteenpence offered by the king at the shrine of the Saint on the day of his departure, besides a silken cloth borrowed for the occasion from the sacrist and never paid for (178). John must, however, have thought highly of the abbot to summon him over sea in 1203 to confer with him as to the Pope's letter concerning the dispensation of Crusaders from their vows (207).

Samson as an Author.—Once when Jocelin asked why he had been sighing so heavily and was so wakeful at nights, Samson confided to him how greatly he felt the burden of his charge; and on another occasion said that if he had known what it involved, he would, rather than be abbot and lord, have preferred to be keeper of the books, "for this office he had ever desired above all others" (55).

Jocelin hints a polite incredulity; but there are evidences that Samson was fond of books, and was indeed an author. There is a small volume, Titus A viii. in the Cottonian collection, which includes in its contents a work in two books, entitled *De Miraculis Sancti Ædmundi*. From a number of marginal notes, of even date with the fourteenth century text, and which ascribe to Samson, amongst other writers, the authorship of various passages in the great legendary life of St. Edmund in the Bodleian Library (MS. 240), Mr. Arnold arrived at the conclusion that "the writer of the work was unquestionably Abbot Samson." For the evidence the reader is referred to Appendix I. (pages 215-21); but it would appear that the work was written before the date when he became abbot, and perhaps before he had been appointed to any one of the numerous offices in the monastery to which he was from time to time transferred by the capricious Hugh (9).

Whenever any new event was recorded in his patron saint's honour, Samson caused it to be recorded: hence at his desire the episode of Henry of Essex, whom St. Edmund had "confounded in the very hour of battle" (102), was reduced to writing at Reading, and interpolated by some other monk in Jocelin's chronicle.

Samson's Masterfulness.—Samson, like his prototype of Scripture, was a "strong man," and as such he came into constant conflict with those who sought to try conclusions with him, usually to their own regret. From instances innumerable, the following may be selected as typical. At his very first general court of his knights, Thomas of Hastings tried to press the claim of his nephew Henry—a minor—to the hereditary stewardship of the Abbey; but Samson said he would consider the matter when Henry could perform the duties (41). Richard, Earl of Clare, demanded his guerdon of five shillings for the office of Standard-bearer of St. Edmund. Samson retorted that the payment of the money would not inconvenience the Abbey; but there were two other claimants for the post, and Richard must settle first with them. The Earl said he would confer with Roger Bigot his kinsman, "and so the matter was put off even to this day" (86).

Geoffrey Ridel, the Bishop of Ely, sent a blundering messenger to the abbot to ask for timber from woods at Elmswell, meaning Elmsett. Samson assented to the request for Elmswell, and meanwhile sent his foresters to Elmsett and cut down a great quantity of oaks, branding them as the property of the Abbey. The bishop overwhelmed his stupid servant with reproaches, and sent him back to explain. But it was too late, "and the bishop, if he wanted timber, had to get it elsewhere" (107).

Herbert the dean erected a windmill upon the Haberdon, and tried to brazen it out with Samson. But the abbot bade him begone, and told him that before he had come to his house, he should hear what had befallen his mill. Whereupon the trembling dean had the mill pulled down himself, so that when the servants of the sacrist came to the spot, they found their work already done for them (90).

In the domestic quarrel with his monks over the case of Ralph, the gate porter, who had been punished by Robert the prior with the assent of all the monastery, Samson upset the proceedings on his return from London, and, after a violent struggle, got his own way (179-83).

There is a pleasing affectation of impartiality in the case of another Herbert, the junior candidate for the office of Prior, on the much-worried Robert's death in 1200. The monks were conscious that Samson "would seek the advice of each with great show of formality," but that the affair would end as he had all along intended (193). On the day of election the Precentor was egged on by one of the elder brethren in an audible aside to nominate Herbert. Samson behaved as if this was a new light to him, but offered no objection to receive Herbert if the convent willed. And so, after a protestation of his unworthiness, Herbert was elected (196); and Jocelin tried, after these bare-faced proceedings, to recover his equanimity in the porch of the guest-chamber (197).

Samson as an Administrator.—Samson seems to have been something of a financial genius; he certainly freed the monastery from debt, and brought its internal affairs and its landed estates from chaos into order. He was undoubtedly more of an administrator than an ecclesiastic. He obviously enjoyed his ceremonial duties as Commissioner for the King or for the Pope. He went to the siege of Windsor in 1193 in martial array, though Jocelin is constrained to admit that he was "more remarkable there for counsel than for piety" (82). He appeared to be in his highest spirits when he went to Coventry in January, 1198, to help to restore the monks there who had been ejected by their somewhat truculent Bishop, Hugh de Nonant. Samson gave magnificent entertainments at Oxford, where the Commission sat, and "never in his life did he seem so joyful as at that time" (143).

He was fond, too, of country life, spending much time at his manors of Melford and elsewhere, "enclosing many parks, which he replenished with beasts of chase, and keeping a huntsman with dogs," though Jocelin is careful to add that he "never saw him take part in the sport" (43). With some of these dogs Samson appeased Richard's wrath when he flouted the king as to a disputed wardship (149). One of the complaints against him by those who chafed under his rule was that he was fond of betaking himself to his manors, and Jocelin's excuse for him is that "the abbot is more in spirits and in good humour elsewhere than at home" (53). Jocelin took him to task over this, but had a text from Ecclesiasticus hurled at his head, which induced him to "hold his peace henceforth" (54).

With broader outlook than his obedientiaries, Samson recognized the necessity of granting greater freedom to the inhabitants of the town of Bury, and, despite the grumbling of his monks, he gave the burgesses a Charter in 1194 (116). The resentment against him in the monastery ran so high in 1199 that he professed to be afraid of his life (182). Though matters were then patched up, the old feeling of indignation against his concessions to the townsfolk endured, and an occasion for manifesting it arose when, early in 1203, Samson was summoned by King John to advise him on a brief sent by the Pope as to the dispensation of certain Crusaders from their vows. To the undisguised astonishment of Jocelin, Samson sought the advice of the monastery, "a thing he heretofore had seldom done" (207); but he was boldly asked what he proposed to do to get back the lost privileges of the Abbey (210). He was then "weakened by infirmity of body, humbled, and (as was not his wont) timid" (207); and it must be remembered that he was by this time not far short of seventy years of age. He spoke the monks fair, promised redress, and "that upon his return he would co-operate with us in everything, and make just order and disposition, and render to each what was justly his" (211).

Jocelin hints by a quotation from Ovid that there was some apprehension that this promise would remain unfulfilled: and then in Carlyle's words—

Jocelin's Boswellian narrative, suddenly shorn through by the scissors of Destiny, ends. Impenetrable Time-curtains rush down. Monks, Abbot, Hero-Worship, Government, Obedience, Cœur de Lion, and St. Edmund's Shrine, vanish like Mirza's vision; and there is nothing left but a mutilated black ruin amid green botanic expanses.

Epilogue.—As to what happened to Samson after he returned from the visit to his sovereign, we have no information whatever from any known source. Perhaps when he had reached the allotted span of life, he came to feel that the time had arrived to take things more easily, and to be less inelastic in his governance of the Abbey. The last nine years of his chequered life are an absolute blank so far as the available records are concerned, if we except his execution of certain formal documents included in the Suffolk Feet of Fines. But when at last, at the ripe age of 77, he died on the 30th December, 1211, at twilight (*inter lupum et canem*), on the night of the feast of St. Thomas the Martyr, a tenderer feeling towards him obviously existed amongst his monks.

The compiler of the *Annales Sancti Edmundi* (who from the last phrase but one would seem to have been a contemporary) thus records his decease:—

On the sixth day of Christmas, at St. Edmund's, died Samson, of pious memory, the venerable abbot of this place. Who, after he had for thirty years prosperously ruled the Abbey committed to him, and had freed it from a load of debt,—had enriched it with privileges, liberties, possessions, and spacious buildings, and had restored the worship of the church, both internally and externally, in the most ample manner, bidding his last farewell to his sons, by whom the blessed man deserved to be blessed for evermore, while they all were standing by, and gazing with awe at a death which was a cause for admiration, not for regret (*non miserabilem sed mirabilem*), in the fourth year of the interdict rested in peace (Arnold, ii. 19, 20).

"In the fourth year of the Interdict": there is a significance in these words not perhaps immediately apparent. During the last few years of Samson's life, public worship in his beloved abbey was stopped; the altars were stripped, and the church doors closed, in view of the interdict hurled at the recalcitrant John by the Pope in March, 1208. More trying than this to the feelings of the age was the requirement that the dead should be buried in silence and in unconsecrated ground. So Samson was laid by his sorrowing monks in the bosom of mother earth "in pratello," where he remained until after the Interdict was removed in July, 1214. The writer of the *Electio Hugonis* records, in barbarous Latin (Arnold, ii. 85), that on August 9 of that year the sacrist raised the question as to the proper interment of Samson "of venerable memory." The prior (Herbert), the cantor and Master Thomas of Walsingham, with other high officials, thought Samson ought, for greater honour, to be buried in the Abbey church. The sacrist—William of Gravelee, of whose uncompromising character we have had a glimpse before—was alone in resisting this, saying that so long as he had any power in the matter, neither Samson nor any one else should be buried in the church. As the sacrist was the responsible official this objection could apparently not be got over, and so on August 12, 1214, the remains of Samson were exhumed, and reburied in the chapter-house, which in the days of his life had resounded to that eloquence of which Jocelin speaks (62).

What happened to the chapter house after the suppression of the Abbey in 1539 is not known; but it seems probable that when the lead of its roof was stripped off, it was left to crumble to decay by itself, for some recent excavations in the winter of 1902-3 brought to light quantities of beautifully worked stone, granite and marble columns, and fragments of stained glass.

On New Year's Day of this year five stone coffins, each with a skeleton within, and a sixth skeleton (uncoffined) were found under the floor of the chapter-house in the exact positions in which a MS. of circa 1425, now preserved at Douai, records the burial places of Samson, two of his predecessors, and three of his successors as Abbots; and there can be no reasonable doubt therefore that those who, like myself, were privileged to be associated with these excavations, have gazed upon the mortal remains of one of the grandest and most picturesque figures of Angevin times.

I am indebted to many friends for hints and suggestions in the preparation of the Notes in Appendix II., especially to Lord Francis Hervey, Dr. Montague R. James, and Mr. Francis Ford, all three of whom have intimate personal knowledge of Bury St. Edmunds and its history. In addition, Dr. James has been good enough to critically compare the English text of the Chronicle with the Latin original, and has made many valuable improvements, for which my especial thanks are due to him. Mr. R. W. Chambers, M.A., Librarian of University College, has also given me much assistance in the revision of the text in the compilation of the Index.

13A, HANOVER SQUARE, W. *May*, 1903.

And to procede ferthere in this mater, Yf ye list aduertise in your mynde, An exaumplaire and a meror cler, In this story ye shal now seen and fynde. So as I kan, in soth I will nat spare But heer in ordre reherse by wrytyng, Folwyng myn auctours in euery maner thyng, As in substance vpon the lettre in deede, To do plesance to them that shal it reede. JOHN LYDGATE.
(*Harleian MS.* 2278: *lines* 417-20, 426-30.)

CHAPTER I
BURY ABBEY UNDER ABBOT HUGH

THAT which I have heard and seen have I taken in hand to write, which in our days has come to pass in the Church of St. Edmund, from the year when the Flemings were taken captive without the town, at which time I took upon me the religious habit, being the same year wherein prior Hugh was deposed, and Robert made prior in his stead: and I have mingled in my narration some evil deeds by way of warning, and some good by way of profit.

Now, at that time, Hugh the abbot was old, and his eyes were somewhat dim. A pious and kind man was he, a good and religious monk, yet not wise or far-sighted in worldly affairs; one who relied too much on his officers, and put faith in them, rather taking counsel of others than abiding by his own judgment.

To be sure, the Rule and the religious life, and all pertaining thereto were healthy enough in the cloister, but outdoor affairs were badly managed; inasmuch as every one serving under a simple and already aged lord did what he would, not what he should.

The townships of the abbot and all the hundreds were set to farm, the forests were destroyed, the manor houses threatened to fall, everything daily got worse and worse. One resource only the abbot had, and that was to take up moneys on interest, so that thereby he might be able in some measure to keep up the dignity of his house. There befel not a term of Easter or St. Michael, for eight years before his decease, but that one or two hundred pounds at least increased in principal debt; the securities were always renewed, and the interest which accrued was converted into principal.

This laxity descended from the head to the members, from the superior to the subjects. Hence it came to pass that every official of the house had a seal of his own, and bound himself in debt at his own pleasure, to Jews as well as to Christians. Oftentimes silken copes and golden cruetts, and other ornaments of the church, were pledged without the knowledge of the convent. I myself saw a security passed to William Fitz Isabel for one thousand and forty pounds, but I never could learn the consideration or the cause. I also saw another security passed to Isaac, the son of Rabbi Joce, for four hundred pounds, but I know not wherefore. I also saw a third security passed to Benedict, the Jew of Norwich, for eight hundred and eighty pounds; and this was the origin of that debt.

Our parlour was destroyed, and it was given in charge to William the sacrist, will he, nill he, that he should restore it. He privily borrowed from Benedict the Jew forty marks at interest, and gave him a security sealed with a certain seal, which used to hang at the shrine of St. Edmund, wherewith the gilds and letters of fraternity were wont to be sealed: a seal which later on, but alas! too late, was broken by order of the convent. Now, when this debt had increased to one hundred pounds, the Jew came bearing a letter from our lord the King, touching the debt of the sacrist; and then it was that all that had been secret from the abbot and convent was laid bare.

The abbot waxed exceedingly wroth, and wished to depose the sacrist, alleging that he possessed a privilege of our lord the pope, giving him power of deposing William, his sacrist, whensoever it pleased him. Howbeit, some one went to the abbot, and excusing the sacrist, so wheedled the abbot that he permitted a security to be passed to Benedict the Jew for four hundred pounds, payable at the end of four years, namely, for one hundred pounds, which had then already accrued for interest, and also for another hundred pounds, which the same Jew had advanced to the sacrist for the use of the abbot. And the sacrist in full chapter undertook for the whole of that debt to be paid, and a deed was drawn up and sealed with the conventual seal: the abbot dissimulating, and not affixing his own seal, as if that debt was no concern of his.

But at the end of the four years, there were no means of discharging the debt; and then a fresh deed was executed for eight hundred and eighty pounds, payable at set terms, at the rate of eighty pounds a year. Moreover, the same Jew had many other securities of smaller account, and one which was for fourteen years; so this debt alone came to one thousand and two hundred pounds, besides the interest that had accrued.

Now R., the almoner of our lord the King, coming to us, signified to the abbot that such and such information had reached the King concerning such and such debts. Thereupon, after consultation had between the prior and a few others, the almoner was conducted into the chapter house, where all of us being seated, and holding our peace, the abbot said, "Look you, here is the King's almoner, our and your lord and friend, who, moved by the love of God and of St. Edmund, has intimated to us that the King has heard something wrong of us and you, and particularly that the affairs of the church, both internally and externally, are being badly managed; and therefore I desire and command that, upon your vow of obedience, ye state and explain openly how things really are." Hereupon the prior, standing up and speaking as one for all, said that the church was in good order, that the Rule was strictly and religiously observed indoors, and that matters out of doors were carefully and discreetly conducted, save some slight debt, in which ourselves, like our neighbours, were involved; but that, in fact, there was no debt which could embarrass us. The almoner, hearing this, said he was rejoiced that he had heard the testimony of the convent concerning this matter: meaning, what the prior had said.

The very same words the prior upon another occasion used, as did Master Geoffry of Constantine, speaking on behalf of and excusing the abbot, when Richard the archbishop, in virtue of his office as legate, visited our chapter, before we had such exemption as we now enjoy.

I myself, who was at that time a novice, on a convenient occasion, talked these things over with the master who instructed me in the Rule, and to whose care I was committed,—namely, Master Samson, who afterwards became abbot. "What is this," I said, "that I hear? How can you hold your tongue while you see and hear such things, you who are a cloistered monk, and desire not offices, and fear God more than man?" But he answering, said, "My son, the newly burnt child dreads the fire; so it is with me and many others. Hugh, the prior, has been lately deprived of his office and sent into exile; Dennis and Hugh and Roger of Hengham have but lately returned home from exile. Even I, in like manner, was imprisoned, and afterwards sent to Acre, because we spoke for the good of our church, in opposition to the abbot. This is the hour of darkness; this is the time when flatterers rule and are believed, and their might is strengthened, and we can do nothing against it; these things must be borne with for a time. 'Let the Lord look upon it and judge.'"

Now a rumour reached Abbot Hugh that Richard, Archbishop of Canterbury, proposed coming to make a visitation of our church by virtue of his authority as legate; and thereupon the abbot, after consultation, sent to Rome and sought a privilege of exemption from the power of the aforesaid legate. On the messenger's return from Rome there was not wherewith to discharge what he had promised to our lord the pope and the cardinals, except, indeed, under the special circumstances of the case, the cross which was over the high altar, the little image of the Virgin, and the St. John (which images archbishop Stigand had adorned with a vast quantity of gold and silver, and had given to St. Edmund).

There were certain of our convent who, being on terms of intimacy with the abbot, said that the shrine of St. Edmund itself ought to be stripped, as the means of obtaining such a privilege. But these persons did not consider the great peril that the possession of such a privilege might entail; for if there should hereafter be any abbot of ours who chose to waste the possessions of the church, and to despoil his convent, then there would be no one to whom the convent could complain touching the wrongs done by an abbot, as he would have no reason to fear a bishop, archbishop, or legate, and his impunity would lend him the courage to transgress.

In these days the cellarer, as well as other officials, borrowed moneys at interest from Jurnet the Jew (without apprising the convent), upon a security sealed with the above-mentioned seal. Now, when that debt had mounted up to sixty pounds, the convent was summoned to pay the cellarer's debt. The cellarer was deposed, although he said it was hard to deal thus with him, stating that for three years he had entertained in the guest-house by the abbot's orders, whether the abbot were in residence or not, all the guests which the abbot ought himself to entertain, according to the rule of the abbey.

Master Dennis was made cellarer in his stead, and by his circumspection and good management he reduced the debt of sixty pounds to thirty pounds; towards which debt we applied those thirty marks which Benedict of Blakenham gave to the convent for holding the manors of Nowton and Whepsted. But the securities of the Jew have remained with the Jew even to this day, wherein are contained the twenty-six pounds of principal and interest of the cellarer's debt.

Now, on the third day after Master Dennis became cellarer, three knights with their esquires were received in the guest-house that they might there be refreshed, the abbot then being at home, and abiding in his inner chamber; all which, when this great-souled Achilles had heard, not willing to pay toll in his own domain, as the others had done, he rose up and took the key of the cellar, and taking with him those knights to the abbot's hall, and approaching the abbot, said, "My lord, you well know that the rule of the abbey is, that knights and lay folk should be entertained in your hall, if the abbot be at home. I neither will nor can receive those guests whom it belongs to you to entertain; else take back the keys of your cellar, and appoint some other cellarer at your good pleasure." The abbot hearing this, nill he, will he, entertained those knights, and ever afterwards entertained knights and lay folk according to the ancient rule, and so they are still received when the abbot is at home.

Once upon a time, Abbot Hugh, wishing to conciliate Master Samson, appointed him sub-sacrist; and he, often accused, was often transferred from one office to another. At one time he was appointed guest-master, at another time pittance-master, at another time third prior, and again sub-sacrist; and many were then his enemies who afterwards flattered him. But he, not acting as the other officials did, never could be induced to turn flatterer; whereupon the abbot said that he had never seen a man whom he could not bend to his will, except Samson the sub-sacrist.

In the twenty-third year of his abbacy, Abbot Hugh bethought him that he would go to St. Thomas for the purpose of performing his devotions. He had nearly got to the end of his journey, on the morrow of the nativity of the

Blessed Mary, when, near Rochester, he most unhappily fell from his horse, so that his knee-pan was put out and lodged in the ham of his knee. The physicians came about him, and sorely tormented him, but they healed him not. He was brought back to us in a horse-litter, and received with great attention, as was most fitting. What more? His leg mortified, and the disorder mounted to his heart. The pain brought on a tertian fever, and on the fourth fit he expired, and rendered his soul to God on the morrow of St. Brice.

Ere he was dead, everything was snatched away by his servants, so that nothing at all remained in the abbot's house except the stools and the tables, which could not be carried away. There was hardly left for the abbot his coverlet and two quilts, old and torn, which some, who had taken away the good ones, had placed in their stead. There was not even a single article of a penny's worth that could be distributed among the poor for the good of his soul.

The sacrist said it was not his business to have attended to this, alleging that he had furnished the expenditure of the abbot and his household for one whole month, because neither the firmars who held the vills would pay anything before the appointed time, nor would creditors advance anything, seeing that he was sick even unto death.

Luckily, the farmer of Palgrave furnished us with fifty shillings to be distributed among the poor, by reason that he entered upon the farm of Palgrave on that same day. But those very fifty shillings were afterwards again refunded to the King's bailiffs, who demanded the whole farm-rent for the King's use.

CHAPTER II
THE MONKS DISCUSS THE VACANCY

HUGH the abbot being buried, it was ordered in chapter that some one should give intelligence to Ranulf de Glanville, the justiciar of England, of the death of the abbot. Master Samson and Master R. Ruffus, our monks, quickly went beyond seas, to report the same fact to our lord the King, and obtained letters that those possessions and rents of the monastery, which were distinct from those of the abbot, should be wholly in the hands of the prior and convent, and that the remainder of the abbey should be in the hands of the King. The wardship of the abbey was committed to Robert of Cockfield and Robert of Flamville, the steward, who forthwith put by gage and safe pledges all those servants and relatives of the abbot to whom the abbot had, after the commencement of his illness, given anything, or who had taken anything away belonging to the abbot, and also the abbot's chaplain (a monk of the house), whom the prior bailed. Entering into our vestiary, they caused all the ornaments of the church to be noted down in an inventory.

During the vacancy in the abbacy, the prior, above all things, studied to keep peace in the convent, and to preserve the honour of the church in entertaining guests, being desirous of irritating no one, of not provoking anybody to anger; in fact, of keeping all persons and things in quietude. He nevertheless winked at some acts in our officials which needed reformation, and especially in the sacrist, as if he cared not how that officer dealt with the sacristy. Yet during the vacancy, the sacrist neither satisfied any debt nor erected any building, but the oblations and incomings were foolishly frittered away.

Wherefore the prior, who was the head of the convent, seemed by the greater part to be highly censurable, and was said to be remiss; and this thing our brethren called to mind among themselves, when it came to the point of making choice of an abbot.

Our cellarer entertained all guests, of whatsoever condition they were, at the expense of the convent. William the sacrist, on his part, gave and spent as he chose, kind man! giving alike what he should and should not; "blinding the eyes of all with gifts."

Samson the sub-sacrist, being master over the workmen, did his best that no breach, chink, crack or flaw should be left unrepaired so far as he was able; whereby he acquired great favour with the convent, and especially with the cloister monks. In those days our choir was erected by Samson's exertion; and he arranged the order of the paintings, and composed elegiac verses for them. He also made a great draught of stone and sand for building the great tower of the church. Being asked whence he procured the money for his work, he answered that certain of the burgesses had privily given him moneys for building and completing the tower.

Nevertheless, certain of our brethren said that Warin, a monk of our house and keeper of the shrine, together with Samson the sub-sacrist, had conspired to remove some portion of the offerings to the shrine, in order that they might disburse the same for the necessary purposes of the church, and in particular for the building of the tower; being the more ready to believe this when they saw that the offerings were expended for extraordinary purposes by others, who, to speak plainly, stole them. And these before-named two men, in order to remove from themselves the suspicion of any such pious theft, made a certain hollow trunk, with a hole in the middle or at the top, and fastened with an iron lock. This they caused to be set up in the great church, near the door without the choir, where the common people usually pass, so that persons should put their contributions therein for the building of the tower.

Now William the sacrist had a jealousy of his companion Samson, as had many others who took part with the same William, Christians as well as Jews; the Jews, I say, to whom the sacrist was said to be father and protector, whose protection they indeed enjoyed, having free ingress and egress, and going all over the monastery, rambling about the altars and by the shrine while high mass was being celebrated. Moreover, their moneys were kept safe in our treasury, under the care of the sacrist, and, what was still more improper, their wives with their little ones were lodged in our pittancy in time of war. His enemies or opponents having, therefore, consulted together how they might suddenly overcome Samson, they conferred with Robert of Cockfield and his colleague, who were wardens of the abbey, and persuaded them to this—that they should, on behalf of the King, forbid any one to erect any fabric or building so long as the abbacy was vacant; but that, on the other hand, the moneys from the offerings should be collected, and kept for the purpose of discharging some debt.

And thus was Samson beguiled, and his "strength departed from him," nor could he from thenceforth labour as he had desired. Indeed, his opponents were able to delay, but not annul, his purpose; for having regained his strength, and "pulled down the two pillars," that is, having removed the two wardens of the abbey, upon whom the malice of others relied, the Lord gave him, in process of time, the means of fulfilling his desire of building the aforesaid tower, and of finishing it even as he wished. And so it was, as if it had been said to him from above, "Well done, thou good and faithful servant; thou hast been faithful over a few things, I will make thee ruler over many things."

During the time that the abbacy was vacant we oftentimes, as was our duty, besought God and the holy martyr St. Edmund that they would vouchsafe to us and our church a meet shepherd, thrice every week singing the seven penitential psalms prostrate in the choir, after going forth from chapter. There were some amongst us who, had it been known who was to be abbot, would not have prayed so devoutly.

As concerned the choice of an abbot, assuming the King gave us free election, divers men spoke in divers ways—some publicly, some privately; and "so many men, so many opinions."

One said of another, "That brother is a good monk, a likely person; he is well conversant with the Rule and custom of the house; although he may not be so perfect a philosopher as certain others, he would make a very good abbot. Abbot Ording was not a learned man, and yet he was a good abbot, and governed this house wisely: we read, too, in the fable, that it had been better for the frogs to have chosen a log for a king, upon whom they might rely, than a serpent, who venomously hissed, and after his hisses devoured his subjects."

Another would answer, "How may this be? How can an unlearned man deliver a sermon in chapter, or to the people on festivals? How can he who does not understand the Scriptures attain the knowledge of 'binding and loosing'? seeing that the cure of souls is the art of arts and science of sciences. God forbid that a dumb image should be set up in the Church of St. Edmund, where many learned and studious men are well known to be."

Also said one of another, "That brother is a good clerk, eloquent and careful, strict in the Rule; he has much loved the convent, and has undergone many hardships in respect of the possessions of the church: he is worthy to be made abbot." Another answered, "From good clerks, Good Lord, deliver us: that it may please Thee to preserve us from the barrators of Norfolk, we beseech Thee to hear us, good Lord." Moreover, one said of another, "That brother is a good manager, which is proved from his department, and from the offices which he has well served, and by the buildings and reparations which he has performed. He is able to travail for and defend the house, and is, moreover, something of a clerk, although 'much learning has not made him mad': he is worthy to be made abbot." Another answered, "God forbid that a man who can neither read nor chant, nor perform Divine service—a wicked and unjust man, and a grinder of the faces of the poor—should be abbot."

Also said one of another, "That brother is a kind man, affable and amiable, peaceful and well-regulated, open-hearted and liberal, a learned man and an eloquent, a proper man enough in looks and deportment, and beloved by many, indoors as well as out; and such a man might, with God's permission, become abbot to the great honour of the church." The other answered, "It is no honour, but rather a burden, to have a man who is too nice in his meat and drink; who thinks it a virtue to sleep long; who is expert in spending much, and yet gets little; who is snoring when others are awake; who always is desirous to be in plenty, nor yet cares for the debts which increase from day to day, nor considers the means of discharging expenses; hating anxiety and trouble; caring for nought so long as one day comes and another goes; a man cherishing and fostering flatterers and liars; a man who is one thing in name and another in deed. From such a prelate defend us, O Lord!"

Also said a certain one of his fellow, "That man is almost wiser than all of us put together, both in secular and ecclesiastical matters; a wonderful counsellor, strict in rule, learned and eloquent, and of proper stature; such a prelate would do honour to our church."

The other answered, "True, if he were of known and approved reputation. His character is questionable; report may lie, or it may not. And although the man you mean is wise, of lowly carriage in chapter, devout in psalmody, strict in the cloister whilst he is in the cloister, yet it is mere outward show with him. What if he do excel in any office? He is too scornful, lightly esteems the monks, is closely intimate with secular persons; and should he be angry, scarcely returns an answer with a good grace to any brother, or to one even asking a question of him."

I heard in like manner one brother disparaged by some, because he was slow of speech; of whom it was said that he had paste or malt in his mouth when he was called upon to speak. And as for myself, being at that time a youth, "I understood as a youth, I spoke as a youth;" and said I never could consent that any one should be made abbot unless he knew somewhat of dialectics, and knew how to discern truth from falsehood. Again, a certain person, who in his own eyes seemed very wise, said, "May the almighty Lord bestow on us a foolish and simple shepherd, so that it should be the more needful for him to get help from us!"

I heard in like manner a certain studious and learned man, and honourable by the nobility of his family, disparaged by some of our seniors merely for this reason—because he was a novice. The novices, on the other hand, said of the elders, that old men were valetudinarians, by no means fit to govern a monastery. And thus many persons spoke many things, "and each was fully persuaded in his own mind."

I observed Samson the sub-sacrist as he was sitting along with the others at blood-letting season (at which time monks are wont to reveal to each other the secrets of the heart, and to talk over matters with each other). I saw him, I say, sitting along with the others, smiling and saying nothing, but noting the words of each, and after a lapse of twenty years calling to mind some of the before-written opinions. In whose hearing I used to reply to these critics, that if we were to put off the choice of an abbot until we found one who was above disparagement or fault, we never should find such a one, for no one alive is without fault, and "no estate is in all respects blessed."

Upon one particular occasion I was unable to restrain myself but must needs blurt out my own private opinion, thinking that I spoke to trusty ears. I then said that a certain person who formerly had a great regard for me, and had conferred many benefits upon me, was unworthy of the abbacy, and that another was more worthy; in fact, I named one for whom I had less regard.

I spoke according to my own conscience, rather considering the common weal of the church than my own advancement; and what I said was true, as the sequel proved. And, behold, one of the sons of Belial disclosed my saying to my friend and benefactor; for which reason, even to this day, never could I since, neither by entreaty nor good offices, regain his goodwill to the full. "What I have said I have said." "And the word once spoken flies without recall."

One thing remains, that I take heed to my ways for the future; and if I should live so long as to see the abbacy vacant, I shall consider carefully what, to whom, and when I speak on such a matter, lest I either offend God by lying, or man by speaking unreasonably. I shall then advise (should I last so long), that we choose not too good a monk, nor yet an over-wise clerk, neither one too simple nor too weak; lest, if he be over wise in his own conceit, he may be too confident in his own judgment, and contemn others; or, if he be too boorish, he may become a byword to others; I know that it has been said, "In the middle you will be safest," also that "Blessed are they who hold a middle course."

Perhaps, after all, it may be the best course to hold my peace altogether, and say in my heart, "He that is able to receive it, let him receive it."

The abbacy being vacant, Augustine, the Archbishop of Norway, took up his abode with us, in the house of the abbot, receiving by the King's precept ten shillings a day from the revenues of the abbey. He was of considerable assistance in obtaining for us our free election, bearing witness of what was well, and publicly declaring before the King what he had seen and heard.

At that time the holy child Robert suffered martyrdom, and was buried in our church; and many signs and wonders were wrought among the people, as we have elsewhere written.

CHAPTER III
THE CHOICE OF A NEW ABBOT

ONE year and three months having elapsed since the death of Abbot Hugh, the King commanded by his letters that our prior and twelve of the convent, in whose mouth the judgment of our body might agree, should appear on a certain day before him, to make choice of an abbot. On the morrow, after the receipt of the letters, we all of us met in chapter for the purpose of discussing so important a matter. In the first place the letters of our lord the King were read to the convent; next we besought and charged the prior, at the peril of his soul, that he would, according to his conscience, name twelve who were to accompany him, from whose life and conversation it might be depended upon that they would not swerve from the right; who, acceding to our charge, by the dictation of the Holy Ghost named six from one side and six from the other side of the choir, and without gainsaying satisfied us on this point. From the right-hand choir were named—Geoffrey of Fordham, Benedict, Master Dennis, Master Samson the sub-sacrist, Hugh the third prior, and Master Hermer, at that time a novice; from the left-hand side—William the sacrist, Andrew, Peter de Broc, Roger the cellarer, Master Ambrose, Master Walter the physician.

But one said, "What shall be done if these thirteen cannot agree before our lord the King in the choice of an abbot?" A certain one answered that that would be to us and to our church a perpetual shame. Therefore, many were desirous that the choice should be made at home before the rest departed, so that by this forecast there should be no disagreement in the presence of the King. But that seemed a foolish and inconsistent thing to do, without the King's assent; for as yet it was by no means a settled thing that we should be able to obtain a free election from the King.

Then said Samson the sub-sacrist, speaking by the spirit of God, "Let there be a middle course, so that from either side peril may be avoided. Let four confessors be chosen from the convent, together with two of the senior priors of the convent, men of good reputation, who, in the presence of the holy relics, shall lay their hands upon the Gospels, and choose amongst themselves three men of the convent most fit for this office, according to the rule of St. Benedict, and put their names into writing. Let them close up that writing with a seal, and so being closed up, let it be committed to us who are about to go to the court. When we shall have come before the King, and it shall appear that we are to have a free election, then, and not till then, shall the seal be broken, and so shall we be sure as to the three who are to be nominated before the King. And let it be agreed amongst us, that in case our lord the King shall not grant to us one of ourselves, then the seal shall be brought back intact, and delivered to the six under oath, so that this secret of theirs shall remain for ever concealed, at the peril of their souls." In this counsel we all acquiesced, and four confessors were then named; namely, Eustace, Gilbert of Alveth, Hugh the third prior, Anthony, and two other old men, Thurstan and Ruald. Which being done, we went forth chanting "Verba mea," and the aforesaid six remained behind, having the rule of St. Benedict in their hands; and they fulfilled that business as it had been pre-ordained.

Now, whilst these six were treating of their matter, we were thinking differently of different candidates, all of us taking it for granted that Samson would be one of the three, considering his travails and perils of death in his journey to Rome for the advancement of our church, and how he was badly treated and put in irons and imprisoned by Hugh the abbot, merely for speaking for the common weal; for he could not be induced to flatter, although he might be forced to hold his tongue.

After some delay, the convent being summoned returned to chapter; and the old men said they had done as they were commanded. Then the prior asked, "How shall it be if our lord the King will not receive any of those three who are nominated in the writing?" And it was answered that whomsoever our lord the King should be willing to accept should be adopted, provided he were a professed monk of our house. It was further added, that if those thirteen brethren should see anything that ought to be amended by another writing, they should so amend it by common assent or counsel.

Samson the sub-sacrist, sitting at the feet of the prior, said, "It will be profitable for the church if we all swear by the word of truth that upon whomsoever the lot of election shall fall, he should treat the convent according to reason, nor change the chief officers without the assent of the convent, nor surcharge the sacrist, nor admit any one to be a monk without assent of the convent." And to this we all of us assented, holding up our right hands in token of assent. It was, moreover, provided, that if our lord the King should desire to make a stranger our abbot, such person should not be adopted by the thirteen, unless upon counsel of the brethren remaining at home.

Upon the morrow, therefore, those thirteen took their way to court. Last of all was Samson, the purveyor of their charges, because he was sub-sacrist, carrying about his neck a little box, in which were contained the letters of the convent—as if he alone was the servant of them all—and without an esquire, bearing his frock in his arms, and going out of the court, he followed his fellows at a distance.

In their journey to the court, the brethren conversing all together, Samson said that it would be well if they all swore that whosoever should be made abbot should restore the churches of the lordships belonging to the convent to the purposes of hospitality; whereto all agreed, save the prior, who said, "We have sworn enough already; you may so restrict the abbot that is to be, that I shall not care to obtain the abbacy." Upon this occasion they swore not at all, and it was well they did so, for had they sworn to this, the oath would not have been observed.

On the very day that the thirteen departed we were all sitting together in the cloister, when William of Hastings, one of our brethren, said, "I know that we shall have one of our convent to be abbot." And being asked how he came to be so certain of this, he replied, that he had beheld in a dream a prophet clothed in white, standing before the gates of the monastery, and that he asked him, in the name of God, whether we should have an abbot of our own. And the prophet answered, "You shall have one of your own body, but he shall rage among you as a wolf"; of which dream the interpretation followed in part, because the future abbot cared more to be feared than loved, as many were accustomed to say.

There also sat along with us another brother, Edmund by name, who asserted that Samson was about to be abbot, and told a vision he had seen the previous night. He said he beheld in his dream Roger the cellarer and Hugh the third prior, standing before the altar, and Samson in the midst, taller by the shoulders upward, wrapt round with a long gown down to his feet, looped over his shoulders, and standing as a champion ready to do battle. And, as it seemed to him in his dream, St. Edmund arose from his shrine, and, as if sickly, showed his feet and legs bare. When some one approached and desired to cover the feet of the saint, the saint said, "Approach me not; behold, he shall veil my feet," pointing with his finger towards Samson. This is the interpretation of the dream: By his seeming to be a champion is signified that the future abbot should always be in travail; at one time moving a controversy against the Archbishop of Canterbury, concerning pleas of the Crown, at another time against the knights of St. Edmund, to compel them to pay their escuages in full; at another time with the burgesses for standing in the market; at another time with the sokemen for the suits of the hundreds; even as a champion who willeth by fighting to overcome his adversaries that he may be able to gain the rights and liberties of his church. And he veiled the feet of the holy martyr when he perfectly completed the towers of the church, commenced a hundred years before.

Such dreams as these did our brethren dream, which were immediately published throughout the cloister, afterwards through the court lodge, so that before the evening it was a matter of common talk amongst the townsfolk, they saying this man and that man are elected, and one of them will be abbot.

At last the prior and the twelve that were with him, after many fatigues and delays, stood before the King at Waltham, the manor of the Bishop of Winchester, upon the second Sunday in Lent. The King graciously received them; and, saying that he wished to act in accordance with the will of God and the honour of our church, commanded the brethren by prolocutors— namely, Richard the Bishop of Winchester, and Geoffrey the chancellor, afterwards Archbishop of York—that they should nominate three members of our convent.

The prior and brethren retiring as if to confer thereupon, drew forth the sealed writing and opened it, and found the names written in this order— Samson, sub-sacrista; Roger, celerarius; Hugo, tercius prior. Hereupon those brethren who were of higher standing blushed with shame; they also marvelled that this same Hugh should be at once elector and elected. But, inasmuch as they could not alter what was done, by mutual arrangement they changed the order of the names; first naming Hugh, because he was third prior; secondly, Roger the cellarer; thirdly, Samson, thus literally making the last first and the first last.

The King, first inquiring whether they were born in his realm, and in whose lordship, said he knew them not, directing that with those three, some other three of the convent should be nominated. This being assented to, William the sacrist said, "Our prior ought to be nominated because he is our head," which was directly allowed. The prior said, "William the sacrist is a good man"; the like was said of Dennis, and that was settled. These being nominated before the King without any delay, the King marvelled, saying, "These men have been speedy in their work; God is with them."

Next the King commanded that, for the honour of his kingdom, they should name three persons of other houses. On hearing this, the brethren were afraid, suspecting some craft. At last, upon conference, it was resolved that they should name three, but upon this understanding, that they would not receive any one of those three, unless by assent of the convent at home. And they named these three—Master Nicholas of Waringford, afterwards (for a season) Abbot of Malmesbury; Bertrand, Prior of St. Faith's, afterwards Abbot of Chertsey; and Master H. of St. Neot's, a monk of Bec, a man highly religious, and very circumspect in spiritual as well as temporal affairs.

This being done, the King thanked them, and ordered that three should be struck off of the nine; and forthwith the three strangers were struck off, namely, the Prior of St. Faith's, afterwards Abbot of Chertsey, Nicholas, a monk of St. Albans, afterwards Abbot of Malmesbury, and the Prior of St. Neot's. William the sacrist voluntarily retired, two of the five were struck out by command of the King, and, ultimately, one out of the remaining three. There then remained but two, the prior and Samson.

Then at length the before-named prolocutors of our lord the King were called to the council of the brethren: and Dennis, speaking as one for all, began by commending the persons of the prior and Samson, saying, that each of them was learned, each was good, each was of meritorious life and good character. But always in the corner of his discourse he gave prominence to Samson, multiplying words in his praise, saying that he was a man strict in life, severe in reforming excesses, and ready to work hard; heedful, moreover, in secular matters, and approved in various offices. The Bishop of Winchester replied, "We see what it is you wish to say; from your address we gather that your prior seems to you to have been somewhat remiss, and that, in fact, you wish to have him who is called Samson." Dennis answered, "Either of them is good, but, by God's help, we desire to have the best." To whom the bishop, "Of two good men the better should be chosen. Speak out at once; is it your wish to have Samson?" Whereupon several, in fact the majority, answered clearly, "We do wish Samson." No one gainsaid this, though some studiously held their peace, being fearful of offending either one or the other.

Samson was then named to the King, and after a brief consultation with those about him, the King called all in, and said, "You present to me Samson—I know him not; had you presented to me your prior, I should have accepted him, because I know and am well acquainted with him; but now I will do as you desire me. Take heed to yourselves; by the very eyes of God, if you have done ill, I shall call you to severe account." And he inquired of the prior, whether he assented to this choice and agreed thereto; who replied that he was well content it should be so, and that Samson was worthy of a much greater dignity.

Then the elect, falling down at the King's feet and kissing them, hastily arose, and forthwith went towards the altar, erect in gait, and with unmoved countenance, singing "Miserere mei Deus," together with his brethren.

The King, observing this, said to the bystanders, "By the eyes of God, this abbot-elect thinks himself worthy to govern an abbey!"

CHAPTER IV
SAMSON'S INSTALLATION

NOW when the news of the election arrived at the monastery, it gladdened all the cloister monks and some of the officers also, but only a few. "It is well," many said, "because it is well." Others said, "Not so; verily we are all deceived." The elect, before he returned to us, received his benediction from my lord of Winchester, who, at the same time, placing the mitre on the head of the abbot, and the ring on his finger, said, "This is the dignity of the abbots of St. Edmund; my experience long since taught me this." The abbot, therefore, keeping three monks with him, despatched the others homewards, sending word by them of his intended arrival on Palm Sunday, and giving charge to certain of them to provide the things necessary for his day of festival.

As he returned homewards, a multitude of new relations came about him offering to serve him, but he answered all of them that he was content with the servants of the prior, nor could he retain others until he had obtained the assent of the convent. Nevertheless, he retained one knight who was well spoken and learned in the law, not so much upon the score of relationship, but on account of his usefulness, he being well practised in secular suits.

This knight he took, while he was fresh to the work, as an assessor in secular controversies; for he was a new abbot, and inexperienced in such concerns, as he himself was free to declare: indeed, before he received the abbacy, he had never been present where gage and safe pledge had been given.

With the accustomed honours, and with a procession, was he received by his convent on Palm Sunday. The abbot's reception was in this wise: overnight he lay at Kentford, and we, at the proper moment, went forth from the chapter-house to meet him with great solemnity, up to the gate of the cemetery, with ringing of bells inside the choir and without. He himself was surrounded by a multitude of men, and when he espied the fraternity, he dismounted from his horse outside the threshold of the gate. Causing his shoes to be taken off, he was received barefooted within the door, and conducted on each side by the prior and sacrist.

We chanted the responses "Benedictus Dominus," in the office of the Trinity, and then "Martyri adhuc," in the office of St. Edmund, leading the abbot up to the high altar. This being finished, the organs and bells were silenced, and the prayer, "Omnipotens sempiterne Deus miserere huic," was said by the prior over the abbot, who was prostrate. An offering was then made by the abbot, and kissing the shrine, he returned into the choir. There

Samson the precentor took him by the hand and led him to the abbot's throne at the west end; where, the abbot still standing, the precentor straightway began, "Te Deum laudamus," and whilst this was being sung, the abbot was kissed by the prior and the whole convent in order. This done, the abbot proceeded to the chapter-house, the whole convent following him, with many others.

"Benedicite" having been said, in the first place he gave thanks to the convent that they had chosen him—who was, he said, the least of them all—to be their lord and shepherd, not on account of his own merits, but solely by the will of God. And beseeching them briefly that they would pray for him, he addressed his discourse to the clerks and knights, requiring them that they should assist him with their advice according to the burden of the charge entrusted to him. And Wimer the sheriff, answering for them all, said, "We are ready to stand by you in counsel and assistance on every occasion, as we did by our dear lord whom God has called to his glory, and to the glory of the holy martyr St. Edmund." And then were the charters of the King concerning the gift of the abbacy produced and read in full audience. Lastly, after a prayer by the abbot himself, that God might guide him according to his Divine grace, and "Amen" being responded by all, he retired to his chamber, spending his day of festival with more than a thousand dinner guests with great rejoicing.

While these things were taking place I was the prior's chaplain, and within four months was made the abbot's chaplain, noting many things, and committing them to memory. On the morrow of his feast the abbot called to him the prior and some few besides, as if seeking advice from others, though he himself knew what he would do. He said that a new seal should be made with a mitred effigy of him, although his predecessors had not the like; but for a time he used the seal of our prior, subscribing at the end of all letters, that he had no seal of his own and therefore he used for the time that of the prior.

Afterwards, setting his household in order, he appointed divers servants to various duties, saying that he had decided to have twenty-six horses in his courtyard, and that a child must first creep and then stand upright and walk. He enjoined this to his servants beyond all things, that they should take heed that in his new state he be not dishonoured by a lack of meat and drink, but rather that they in all things should anxiously provide for the hospitality of the house. In ordering and appointing these and all other things, he fully relied upon God's providence and his own understanding, and judged it beneath him to require counsel at another's hand as if he were not able to look after his own affairs.

The monks marvelled, the knights were discontented, accusing him of arrogance, and, in some measure censuring him at the King's court, saying that he refused to govern according to the advice of his own freemen. As for him, he removed from his own private counsel the heads of the abbey, lay as well as clerical; indeed, all those without whose advice and assistance the abbey, as it seemed, could not be governed. By reason of this circumstance, Ranulf de Glanville, Justiciary of England, at first held him in distrust, and was less gracious to him than was fitting, until it was made clear, by good evidence, that the abbot had been acting with due caution and prudence in respect of indoor as well as external matters.

A general court having been summoned, all the barons, knights and freemen appeared to do homage on the fourth day of Easter; when, behold, Thomas of Hastings, with a great multitude of knights, came introducing Henry his nephew, not yet a knight, claiming the stewardship with its perquisites, according to the tenor of his charter. To whom the abbot replied, "I do not refuse Henry his right, nor do I wish so to do. If he were competent to serve me in his own person, I would assign him necessaries for ten men and eight horses in my own court-lodge, according to the tenor of his charter. If you present to me a steward, his deputy, who is competent and able to perform the duty, I will receive him in the same manner as my predecessor retained him at the time of his decease, namely, with four horses and their appurtenances. And if this does not content you, I shall carry the plaint before the King or his chief justice." Hereupon the business was deferred.

Ultimately there was presented to him a simple and foolish steward, Gilbert by name, of whom, before he received him into his household, he spoke to his friends as follows: "If there be a default in the administration of the King's justice through the unskilfulness of the steward, he will be in mercy of the King, and not I, for this, that he claims the office by hereditary right; and therefore I had much rather receive him for the present than a sharper witted man to deceive me. By God's assistance I trust I shall be my own steward."

After receipt of the homages, the abbot sued for an aid from the knights, who promised each twenty shillings; but immediately they took counsel together and withheld twelve pounds in respect of twelve knights, alleging that those twelve ought to assist the other forty in keeping their castle-guards, and for their escuages, as well as in respect of the abbot's aid. The abbot, hearing this, waxed wroth, and said to his intimate friends that if he lived long enough he would give them turn for turn and wrong for wrong.

CHAPTER V
THE NEW ABBOT'S REFORMS

AFTER these things the abbot caused inquisition to be made throughout each manor, concerning the annual quit rents from the freemen, and the names of the labourers and their tenements, and the services due from each; and he reduced all into writing. Likewise he repaired those old halls and unroofed houses round which hovered kites and crows. He built new chapels, and likewise inner chambers and upper stories in many places where there never had been any dwelling-house at all, but only barns. He also enclosed many parks, which he replenished with beasts of chase, keeping a huntsman with dogs; and, upon the visit of any person of quality, sat with his monks in some walk of the wood, and sometimes saw the coursing of the dogs; but I never saw him take part in the sport.

He cleared much land, and brought it into tillage, in all things looking forward to the benefit likely to accrue to the abbey; but I wish he had been equally careful in assigning the manors of the convent. Nevertheless, he, for a time, kept our manors of Bradfield and Rougham in hand, making up the deficiencies of the rents by the expenditure of forty pounds. These he afterwards reassigned to us when he heard that dissatisfaction was expressed in the convent, on account of his keeping our manors in his own hand. Likewise in managing these manors, as well as in all other matters, he appointed keepers who were far more careful than their predecessors—some monks, some laymen, to look after us and our lands more carefully.

He also held the eight hundreds in his own hand, and, after the death of Robert of Cockfield, he took in hand the hundred of Cosford, all which he committed to the keeping of those servants who were of his own table; referring matters of greater moment to his own decision, and deciding by means of others upon matters of lesser import—indeed, wringing everything to his own profit.

Moreover, by his command, a general survey was made throughout the hundreds of the leets and suits, of hidages and foddercorn, of hen-rents, and of other dues and rents and issues, which, for the greater part, had ever been concealed by the farmers. He reduced it all to writing, so that within four years from the time of his election, there was not one who could defraud him of the rents of the abbey to the value of a single penny, whereas he himself had not received from his predecessors any writing touching the management of the abbey, except one small schedule, wherein were the names of the knights of St. Edmund and the names of the manors, and what rent was due on each farm. This book he called his kalendar, wherein also were entered the debts he had satisfied; and this same book he almost daily perused, as if in the same he were beholding the face of his honesty in a glass.

The first day that he held a chapter, he confirmed to us, under his new seal, sixty shillings from Southrey, which his predecessors had unjustly received from Edmund, surnamed the golden monk, for the liberty of holding the same vill to farm all the days of his life. He also proposed, as a general rule, that from thenceforth no one should pledge the ornaments of the church without the assent of the convent, as had been the custom heretofore, nor that any charter should be sealed with the convent seal, unless in chapter in the presence of the convent. He appointed Hugh as sub-sacrist, ordering that William the sacrist should not have anything to do with the sacristy, either in the matter of receipt or disbursement, unless by his consent. After this, but not on the same day, he transferred the former keepers of the offerings to other offices; lastly, he deposed the same William: wherefore those who liked William said, "Behold the abbot! Lo, here is the wolf of whom it was dreamed! See how he rages!"

And some of them would have entered into a conspiracy against the abbot. When this was disclosed to him, he, not caring to be altogether silent, nor yet to disquiet the convent, entered the chapter-house on the morrow, and pulled out a little bag full of cancelled deeds, the seals yet hanging thereto, consisting of the securities, partly of his predecessor, partly of the prior, partly of the sacrist, partly of the chamberlain, and other officials, whereof the total was three thousand and fifty-two pounds and one mark without alloy, besides the interest that had accrued thereupon, the amount of which could never be ascertained. All these he had arranged for within one year after his election, and within twelve years entirely discharged. "Behold," said he, "the good management of William, our sacrist; look at the multitude of securities signed with his seal, whereby he has pledged silken copes, dalmatics, censers of silver and books ornamented with gold, without the knowledge of the convent, all which I have redeemed and have restored to you."

He likewise added many other things, showing why he had deposed the said William: howbeit he suppressed the real cause, not wishing to put him to open shame. And when he put Samson the precentor in his place, a person approved by us, and above all objection, everything was quiet again. Furthermore, the abbot commanded that the houses of the sacrist in the cemetery should be entirely plucked up, as though they were not worthy to stand upon the earth, by reason of the frequent wine-bibbings, and certain other acts not to be named, which he, with grief and indignation, had witnessed while he was sub-sacrist. So completely did he obliterate the whole that, within a year, upon the spot where a noble dwelling had stood, we saw beans growing, and where casks of wine had lain, nettles abounding.

After the end of Easter, the abbot went over every one of his and our manors, as well as over those we had confirmed to the farmers in fee, requiring from all of them aid and acknowledgment, according to the law of the land. Thus every day he was increasing in secular knowledge, and was turning his attention to the learning and method of ordering outdoor affairs. Now when he had come to Warkton, where he slept at night, there came to him a voice saying, "Samson, arise up quickly"; and, again, "Get up without delay." Getting up astonished, he looked around him, and perceived a light in a necessary house, namely, a candle ready to fall down upon the straw, which Reiner the monk had carelessly left there. When the abbot had put it out, going through the house, he perceived the door (which was the sole entrance) so fastened that it could only be opened by a key—likewise the windows fastened: so that if a fire had arisen, he, and all with him, who slept upon that floor, had surely perished, for there was no place whence they might get out or escape.

At that time, wheresoever the abbot went, there came about him Jews as well as Christians, demanding debts, and worrying and importuning him so that he could not sleep. Thereupon he became pale and thin, and was constantly repeating, "My heart will never rest until I know the extent of my debts." The feast of St. Michael being come, he took all his manors into his own hand, with but small store of live or dead stock; he freely forgave Walter of Hatfield nineteen pounds arrears, that he might absolutely take back four manors which Hugh the abbot had confirmed to him, namely, Hargrave and Saxham and Chevington and Stapleford; Harlow, indeed, the abbot deferred to take to himself on the present occasion.

Once on a time, as we passed through the forest in returning from London, I inquired in the hearing of my lord abbot, from an old woman passing by, whose was this wood, and of what town, who was the lord, and who was the keeper? She answered that the wood belonged to the abbot of St. Edmund, as part of the town of Harlow, and that the name of the keeper was Arnald. When I inquired further, how Arnald conducted himself towards the men of the town, she answered, that he was a devil incarnate, an enemy of God, and one to flay the poor alive; but now, she added, he is afraid of the new abbot of St. Edmund, whom he believes to be prudent and vigilant, and therefore he treats the men gently. On hearing this, the abbot was delighted, and deferred taking to the manor for a season.

At that time there came unexpectedly the news of the death of the wife of Herlewin of Rungton, who had a charter to hold the same town for her life; and the abbot said, "Yesterday, I would have given sixty marks to have freed the manor from this incumbrance, but now God has freed it." And as he was going thither without delay, that he might take that town into his own hand, and on the morrow was going to Tillener, a part of that manor, there came a certain knight offering thirty marks for the tenure of that carucate of land, with the appurtenances, by the old rent-service, to wit, four pounds, whereto the abbot could not agree; and he had therefrom in that year twenty-five pounds, and the second year twenty pounds.

These and such like things induced him to hold everything in his own keeping; as it is written elsewhere, "Cæsar was all in all." In the first place, far from being inert, he commenced building barns and byres, above all things solicitous to dress the land for tillage, and watchful in preserving the woods, in respect whereof, either in giving or diminishing, he confessed himself to be a very miser. There was but one manor, and that was Thorpe, which by his charter he confirmed to one of English birth, a villein, whose honesty he trusted the more, as he was a good husbandman, and could not speak French.

Scarcely seven months had elapsed since his election, when, behold! there were presented to him the letters of our lord the Pope, appointing him a judge to determine causes, for the execution of which he was incompetent and inexperienced, although he was thoroughly imbued with liberal arts and divinity, as befitted a man of learning, a literate man, educated in the schools and a master in them, known and approved in his own province. Wherefore he invited two clerks, learned in the law, and associated them to himself. Of their advice he availed himself in ecclesiastical matters, employing himself upon the decrees and decretal epistles, when an opportunity offered; so that within a short time, as well by references to books as by the handling of causes, he became reputed a discreet judge, proceeding in every suit according to form of law; so a certain person said, "Cursed be the court of this abbot, where neither gold nor silver can help me to confound my adversary."

In process of time, becoming somewhat practised in secular causes, and taught by an inborn commonsense, he became of so subtle a wit that all marvelled; indeed, by Osbert Fitz-Hervey, the under-sheriff, it was said, "This abbot is a wrangler; if he goes on as he has begun, he will outwit us all, many as we be." Now the abbot becoming an expert man in causes of this description, was made a justice errant, but yet he preserved himself from error and corruption. But "envy aims at the highest." When his men made their plaints to him in the court of St. Edmund, because he was unwilling to give hasty judgment, or to "believe every spirit," but preferred to proceed in due course of law, well knowing that the merits of causes are developed by the allegations of the parties, it was said of him that he would not do justice to any complainant, unless by the intervention of money given or promised.

Because his aspect was acute and penetrating, with a Cato-like countenance, rarely smiling, it was said that he inclined to severity rather than kindness. In receiving amerciaments for any forfeiture, it was said that

"Mercy rejoices against judgment"; for as it seemed to many, when it became an affair of receiving money, he seldom remitted what by law he was entitled to take.

In like manner as he advanced in wisdom, so did he advance in thoughtful care, in respect of keeping and acquiring property, and in creditably regulating his expenses. But even here many backbiters took their ground, saying that he resorted to the sacristy at his own pleasure, sparing his own purse, letting his corn lie by for a dear season, and taking to his manors in other sort than his predecessors did, charging the cellarer with the entertainment of those guests he himself was bound to receive; so that by this craft it might be said that the abbot was careful and well stocked at the end of the year; while, on the other hand, the convent and officials were to be accounted careless and improvident. In reply to these back-bitings, I used to observe, that if he took anything from the sacrist, he turned it to the good account of the church, and this none of these slanderers could deny. And in good truth, greater and more numerous works were carried out by the help of the offerings to the sacristy within fifteen years after his election than in the forty years before it.

To the other objections, that the abbot was fond of betaking himself to his manors, I was wont to answer, and did excuse him, saying, "The reason is because the abbot is more in spirits and in good humour elsewhere than at home." And this was true enough, whether it were by reason of the frequency of suitors who came about him, or from the tale-bearers, wherefore it frequently happened that by the appearance of severity in his face he lost much favour and grace in the eyes of his guests, notwithstanding they fared well in eating and drinking. I noticed this, and took an opportunity, when I was with him in private, to say, "There are two things in which I am much surprised at you." When he had inquired what these things might be, "One is that in spite of your position you still encourage the doctrine of the school of Melun, which says that from a false premiss no conclusion can follow, and other idle sayings."

To which, when he had said his say, I added, "The other indeed is, that when you are at home you do not exhibit the same gracious demeanour you do when elsewhere, nor do you mix in society with those brethren who have a strong regard for you, and have chosen you for their lord; but contrariwise, you seldom associate with them, nor do you, as they say, make yourself on sociable terms with them." Hearing this, he changed countenance, and hanging down his head, said, "You are a simpleton, and speak foolishly; you ought to know what Solomon says—'Hast thou many daughters: show not thyself cheerful toward them.'" I indeed held my peace from thenceforth, setting a watch on my mouth.

On another occasion I said, "My lord, I heard you this night after matins wakeful and sighing heavily, contrary to your usual wont." He answered, "No wonder; you are partaker of my good things, in meat and drink, in riding abroad, and such like, but you have little need to care concerning the conduct of the house and household of the saints, and arduous business of the pastoral care which harasses me and makes my spirit to groan and be heavy." Whereto I, lifting up my hands to heaven, made answer, "From such anxiety, almighty and most merciful Lord, deliver me!"

I have heard the abbot say, that if he could have been as he was before he became a monk, and could have had five or six marks of income wherewith he could have been supported in the schools, he never would have been monk or abbot. On another occasion he said with an oath, that if he could have foreseen what and how great a charge it had been to govern the abbey, he would rather than abbot and lord have been master of the almonry, and keeper of the books, for this office he said he had ever desired above all others. Yet who would credit this? Scarcely myself; and not even myself, except that being constantly with him by day and night for six years, I had had the opportunity of becoming fully conversant with the worthiness of his life and the wisdom of his rule.

He once related to me, that when he was a child of nine years old, he dreamed that he was standing before the gates of the cemetery of the church of St. Edmund, and that the devil, with outspread arms, would have seized him, had not St. Edmund, standing by, taken him in his arms; whereupon he screamed whilst dreaming in his sleep, "St. Edmund, save me!" and thus calling upon him whose name he had never heard, he awoke. His mother was alarmed at such an outcry, but having heard the dream, took him to St. Edmund for the purpose of praying there; and when they had come to the gate of the cemetery he said, "See, mother, this is the place, this is the very same gate which I saw in my dream when the devil was about to seize me"; and he knew the place as well, to use his own words, as if he had seen it before with his natural eyes. The abbot himself interpreted this dream thus: By the devil were signified the pleasures of this mortal state, which would fain have drawn him away; but St. Edmund threw his arms around him when he made him a monk.

Once when he was told that certain of the convent grumbled at some act of his, he said to me as I sat by him, "Good God! there is need enough that I should remember that dream wherein it was dreamed of me, before I was made abbot, that I was to rage among them as a wolf. True it is that above all earthly things I dread lest the convent behave in such a way that I shall be compelled so to rage. But even so it is, when they say or do anything against my will, I bring to mind that dream of theirs, and although I do rage in my own soul, growling and gnashing my teeth in secret, I do violence to myself lest I should actually rage in word or deed," and "My hidden grief chokes me and my heart surges within me."

Although by nature he was quick to wrath, and easily kindled to anger, yet with a great struggle he mostly restrained his temper in view of the dignity he held. Concerning which he sometimes used to boast, "This and that I saw, this and that I heard, yet I held my peace." The abbot once said, seated in chapter, certain words by which he seemed to eagerly desire the good-will of the monastery. "I do not wish," he said, "that any one should come to me to accuse another, unless he is willing to say the same openly. If any one does otherwise, I will publicly proclaim the name of the accuser. I wish also that every cloister monk shall have free access to me, that he may speak to me, whenever he chooses, concerning all things necessary to him." This he said, because our leaders in the days of Abbot Hugh, wishing that nothing should be done in the monastery except through them, had decreed that no cloister monk should speak with the abbot unless he had first told the abbot's chaplain what he wished to speak about.

On a certain day he made an order in chapter, that every one who had a seal of his own should give it up to him, and so it was accordingly done, and there were found three-and-thirty seals. He himself explained the reason of this order, forbidding that any official should incur any debt above twenty shillings without the assent of the prior and convent, as had been the custom heretofore. To the prior and to the sacrist, indeed, he returned their seals, but kept the rest himself.

At another time he ordered to be delivered up to him all the keys of the chests, cupboards, and hanapers, strictly enjoining that thenceforth none presume to have a chest or anything locked up, unless by special permission, or otherwise possess anything beyond what the rule allows. Notwithstanding this he gave general licence to every one of us to have money to the amount of two shillings, if so much happened to have been given to us by way of charity; so that it might be expended upon poor relations, or for purposes of piety.

On another occasion the abbot said, that he was desirous of adhering to our ancient custom respecting the entertainment of guests; that is, when the abbot is at home, he is to receive all guests of whatsoever condition they may be, except religious and priests of secular habit, and except their men who present themselves at the gate of the court in the name of their masters; but if the abbot be not at home, then all guests of whatsoever condition are to be received by the cellarer up to thirteen horses. But if a layman or clerk shall come with more than thirteen horses, they shall be entertained by the servants of the abbot, either within the court-lodge, or without, at the expense of the abbot. All religious men, even bishops if they happen to be monks, are to be charged upon the cellary and at the expense of the convent, unless the abbot will do any one special honour, and entertain him in his own hall at his own expense.

CHAPTER VI
SAMSON'S PERSONAL CHARACTERISTICS

THE abbot Samson was of middle stature, nearly bald, having a face neither round nor yet long, a prominent nose, thick lips, clear and very piercing eyes, ears of the nicest sense of hearing, arched eyebrows, often shaved; and he soon became hoarse from a short exposure to cold. On the day of his election he was forty and seven years old, and had been a monk seventeen years. He had then a few grey hairs in a reddish beard, and a very few in a black and somewhat curly head of hair. But within fourteen years after his election it became as white as snow.

He was a man remarkably temperate, never slothful, of strong constitution, and willing to ride or walk till old age gained upon him and moderated such inclination. On hearing the news of the Cross being taken, and the loss of Jerusalem, he began to use under garments of horsehair and a horsehair shirt, and to abstain from flesh and flesh meats. Nevertheless, he desired that meats should be placed before him at table for the increase of the alms dish. Sweet milk, honey and such like sweet things he ate with greater appetite than other food.

He abhorred liars, drunkards and talkative folk; for virtue ever is consistent with itself and rejects contraries. He also much condemned persons given to murmur at their meat or drink, and particularly monks who were dissatisfied therewith, himself adhering to the uniform course he had practised when a monk. He had likewise this virtue in himself, that he never changed the mess set before him.

Once when I, then a novice, happened to be serving in the refectory, I wished to prove if this were true, and I thought I would place before him a mess which would have displeased any other than him, in a very black and broken dish. But when he looked at it, he was as one that saw it not. Some delay took place, and I felt sorry that I had so done; and snatching away the dish, I changed the mess and the dish for a better, and brought it to him; but this substitution he took in ill part, and was angry with me for it.

An eloquent man was he, both in French and Latin, but intent more on the substance and method of what was to be said than on the style of words. He could read English books most admirably, and was wont to preach to the people in English, but in the dialect of Norfolk, where he was born and bred; and so he caused a pulpit to be set up in the church for the ease of the hearers, and for the ornament of the church. The abbot also seemed to prefer an active life to one of contemplation, and rather commended good officials than good monks. He very seldom approved of any one on account of his literary acquirements, unless he also possessed sufficient knowledge of secular matters; and whenever he chanced to hear that any prelate had resigned his pastoral care and become an anchorite, he did not praise him for it. He never applauded men of too compliant a disposition, saying, "He who endeavours to please all, ought to please none."

In the first year of his being abbot, he appeared to hate all flatterers, and especially among the monks; but in process of time it seemed that he heard them more readily, and was more familiar with them. It once happened that a certain brother of ours, skilled in this art, had bent the knee before him, and under the pretence of giving advice, had poured the oil of flattery into his ears. I, standing apart, smiled. The brother having departed, I was called and asked why I had smiled. I answered, "The world is full of flatterers." And the abbot replied, "My son, it is long that I have known flatterers; I cannot, therefore, avoid hearing them. There are many things to be passed over and taken no notice of, if the peace of the convent is to be preserved. I will hear what they have to say, but they shall not deceive me if I can help it, as they did my predecessor, who trusted so unadvisedly to their counsel that for a long time before his death he had nothing for himself or his household to eat, unless it were obtained on trust from creditors; nor was there anything to be distributed among the poor on the day of his burial, unless it were the fifty shillings which were received from Richard the farmer, of Palgrave, which very fifty shillings the same Richard on another occasion had to pay to the King's bailiffs, who demanded the entire farm-rent for the King's use." With this saying I was comforted. His study, indeed, was to have a well-regulated house, and enough wherewith to keep his household, so managing that the usual allowance for a week, which his predecessor could not make last for five days, sufficed him for eight, nine or even ten days, if so be that he was at his manors without any extraordinary arrival of guests. Every week, indeed, he audited the expenses of the house, not by deputy, but in his own person, which his predecessor had never been wont to do.

For the first seven years he had only four courses in his house, afterwards only three, except presents and game from his parks, or fish from his ponds. And if at any time he retained any one in his house at the request of a great man, or of a particular friend, or messengers, or minstrels, or any person of that description, by taking the opportunity of going beyond sea or travelling afar off, he prudently disencumbered himself of such hangers-on.

The monks with whom the abbot had been the most intimate, and whom he liked best before he became abbot, he seldom promoted to offices merely for old acquaintance' sake, unless they were fit persons. Wherefore certain of our brethren who had been favourable to his election as abbot, said that he cared less for those who had liked him before he became abbot than was proper, and particularly that those were most favoured by him who both openly and in secret had spoken evil of him, nay, had even publicly called him, in the hearing of many, a passionate unsociable man, a proud fellow, and Norfolk barrator. But on the other hand, as after he had received the abbacy he exhibited no indiscreet partiality for his old friends, so he refrained from showing anything like hatred or dislike to many others according to their deserts, returning frequently good for evil, and doing good to them that persecuted him.

He had this way also, which I have never observed in any other man, that he had an affectionate regard for many to whom he seldom or never showed a countenance of love; according to the common proverb which says, "Where love is, there is the regard of love." And another thing I wondered at in him was, that he knowingly suffered loss in his temporal matters from his own servants, and confessed that he winked at them; but this I believe to have been the reason, that he might watch a convenient opportunity when the matter could be advisedly remedied, or that by passing over these matters without notice, he might avoid a greater loss.

He loved his kinsmen indifferently, but not less tenderly than others, for he had not, or assumed not to have, any relative within the third degree. I have heard him state that he had relations who were noble and gentle, whom he never would in any wise recognize as relations; for, as he said, they would be more a burden than an honour to him, if they should happen to find out their relationship. But he always acknowledged those as kinsmen who had treated him as such when he was a poor monk. Some of these relations (that is, those whom he found useful and suitable) he appointed to various offices in his own house, others he made keepers of manors. But those whom he found unworthy, he irrevocably dismissed from his presence.

A certain man of lowly station, who had managed his patrimony faithfully, and had served him devotedly in his youth, he looked upon as his dearest kinsman, and gave to his son, who was a clerk, the first church that fell vacant after he came to the charge of the abbey, and also advanced all the other sons of this man.

He invited to him a certain chaplain who had maintained him in the schools of Paris by the sale of holy water, and bestowed upon him an ecclesiastical benefice sufficient for his maintenance by way of vicarage. He granted to a certain servant of his predecessor food and clothing all the days of his life, he being the very man who put the fetters upon him at his lord's command when he was cast into prison. To the son of Elias, the cupbearer of Hugh the abbot, when he came to do homage for his father's land, he said, in full court, "I have for these seven years deferred taking your homage for the land which the abbot Hugh gave your father, because that gift was to the damage of the manor of Elmswell. Now I am overcome when I call to my mind what your father did for me when I was in fetters, for he sent to me a portion of the very wine whereof his lord had been drinking, and bade me be strong in God." To Master Walter, the son of Master William of Diss, suing at his grace for the vicarage of the church of Chevington, he replied, "Your father was master of the schools, and at the time when I was a poor clerk he granted me freely and in charity an entrance to his school, and the means of learning; now I, for the sake of God, do grant you what you ask."

He addressed two knights of Risby, William and Norman, at the time when they were adjudged to be in his mercy, publicly in this wise: "When I was a cloister monk, sent to Durham upon business of our church, and thence returning through Risby, being benighted, I sought a night's lodging from Norman, and I received a blank refusal; but going to the house of William, and seeking shelter, I was honourably entertained by him. Now, therefore, those twenty shillings, which are 'the mercy,' I will without mercy exact from Norman; but contrariwise, to William I give thanks, and the amerciament of twenty shillings that is due from him I do with pleasure remit."

A certain young girl, seeking her food from door to door, complained to the abbot that one of the sons of Richard, the son of Drogo, had forced her; and at length, by the suggestion of the abbot, for the sake of peace, she took one mark in satisfaction. The abbot, moreover, took from the same Richard four marks for licence to agree; but all those five marks he ordered forthwith to be given to a certain chapman, upon the condition that he should take this poor woman to wife.

In the town of St. Edmund, the abbot purchased stone houses, and assigned them for the use of the schools, so that thereby the poor clerks should be for ever free from house-rent, towards payment whereof all the scholars, whether rich or poor, were compelled twice in the year to subscribe a penny or a halfpenny.

The recovery of the manor of Mildenhall for one thousand and one hundred marks of silver, and the expulsion of the Jews from the town of St. Edmund, and the founding of the new hospital at Babwell, are proofs of great virtue.

The lord abbot sought from the King letters enjoining that the Jews should be driven away from the town of St. Edmund, he stating that whatsoever is within the town of St. Edmund, or within the banlieue thereof, of right belongs to St. Edmund: therefore the Jews ought to become the men of St. Edmund, otherwise they should be expelled from the town. Licence was accordingly given that he might put them forth, saving, nevertheless, that they had all their chattels and the value of their houses and lands. And when they were expelled, and with an armed force conducted to divers towns, the abbot gave order that all those that from henceforth should harbour or entertain Jews in the town of St. Edmund should be solemnly excommunicated in every church and at every altar. Howbeit it was afterwards conceded by the King's justices that if the Jews should come to the great pleas of the abbot to demand their debts from their debtors, on such occasion they might for two days and two nights lodge within the town, and on the third day be permitted to depart freely.

The abbot offered King Richard five hundred marks for the manor of Mildenhall, stating that the manor was worthy sixty and ten pounds by the year, and for so much had been recorded in the great roll of Winchester. And when he had conceived hopes of success in his application, the matter rested till the morrow. In the meanwhile there came a certain person to the King, telling him that this manor was well worth yearly a hundred pounds. On the morrow, therefore, when the abbot urged his suit, the King said, "It is of no avail my lord abbot, what you ask me; you shall either give a thousand marks, or you shall not have the manor." And whereas the Queen Eleanor, according to the custom of the realm, ought to have one hundred marks where the King receives a thousand, she took of us a great gold cup of the value of a hundred marks, and gave us back the same cup for the soul of her lord, King Henry, who first gave the same cup to St. Edmund. On another occasion, when the treasure of our church was carried to London for the ransom of King Richard, the same Queen redeemed that cup for one hundred marks, and restored it to us, taking in return our charter from us as an evidence of our most solemn promise, that we should never again alienate that cup from our church upon any occasion whatever.

Now, when all this money, which was got together with great difficulty, had been paid, the abbot held a chapter, and said he ought to have some portion of the great advantage derivable from so valuable a manor. And the convent answered that it was just, and "Let it be according to your wish." The abbot replied that he could well claim the half part as his own right, demonstrating that he had paid towards this purchase more than four hundred marks, with much inconvenience to himself. But he said that he would be content with a certain allotment of that manor called Icklingham, which was most freely granted him by the convent. When the abbot heard this, he said, "And I do accept this part of the land to my own use, but not that I intend to keep the same in my own hand, or that I shall give it to my relations, but for the good of my soul and for all your souls in common, I give the same to the new hospital at Babwell, for the relief of the poor, and the maintenance of hospitality." As he said, so it was done, and afterwards confirmed by the King's Charter.

These and all other like things worthy to be written down and lauded for ever did the abbot Samson. But he said he had done nothing, unless he could have our church dedicated in his lifetime; which done, he said he wished to die. For the solemnization of this act, he said he was ready to pay two thousand marks of silver, so that the King should be present, and the affair be completed with the reverence it demanded.

The abbot was informed that the church of Woolpit was vacant, Walter of Coutances being chosen to the bishopric of Lincoln. He presently convened the prior and great part of the convent, and taking up his story thus began: "You well know what trouble I had in respect of the church of Woolpit; and in order that it should be obtained for your exclusive use I journeyed to Rome at your instance, in the time of the schism between Pope Alexander and Octavian. I passed through Italy at that time when all clerks bearing letters of our lord the Pope Alexander were taken. Some were imprisoned, some hanged, and some, with nose and lips cut off, sent forward to the pope, to his shame and confusion. I, however, pretended to be Scotch; and putting on the garb of a Scotchman, and the gesture of one, I often brandished my staff, in the way they use that weapon called a gaveloc, at those who mocked me, using threatening language, after the manner of the Scotch. To those that met and questioned me as to who I was, I answered nothing, but, 'Ride ride Rome, turne Cantwereberei.' This did I to conceal myself and my errand, and that I should get to Rome safer in the guise of a Scotchman.

"Having obtained letters from the pope, even as I wished, on my return I passed by a certain castle, as my way led me from the city; and behold the officers thereof came about me, laying hold upon me, and saying, 'This vagabond who makes himself out to be a Scotchman is either a spy or bears letters from the false pope Alexander.' And while they examined my ragged clothes, and my boots, and my breeches, and even the old shoes which I carried over my shoulders, after the fashion of the Scotch, I thrust my hand into the little wallet which I carried, wherein was contained the letter of our lord the pope, placed under a little cup I had for drinking. The Lord God and St. Edmund so permitting, I drew out both the letter and the cup together, so that extending my arm aloft, I held the letter underneath the cup. They could see the cup plain enough, but they did not see the letter; and so I got clear out of their hands, in the name of the Lord. Whatever money I had about me they took away; therefore I had to beg from door to door, without any payment, until I arrived in England.

"But hearing that this church had been given to Geoffrey Ridel, my soul was heavy, because I had laboured in vain. Coming, therefore, home, I crept under the shrine of St. Edmund, fearing lest the abbot should seize and imprison me, although I deserved no punishment; nor was there a monk who durst speak to me, or a layman who durst bring me food except by stealth. At last, upon consideration, the abbot sent me to Acre in exile, and there I remained a long time.

"These and innumerable other things have I endured on account of this church of Woolpit, but, blessed be God, who works all things together, behold! this very church, for which I have borne so many sufferings is given into my hand, and now I have the power of presenting it to whomsoever I will, because it is vacant. And now I restore it to the convent, and I assign to its exclusive use, the ancient custom or pension of ten marks, which you have lost for upwards of sixty years. I had much rather have given it to you entire, could I have done so; but I know that the Bishop of Norwich might gainsay this; or even if he did grant it, he would make it an occasion to claim to himself such subjection and obedience from you as it is not advisable or expedient you should acknowledge. Therefore let us do that which by law we may; that is, put a clerk in as vicar, who shall account to the bishop for the spiritualities, and to yourselves for ten marks. I propose, if you all agree, that this vicarage be given to some kinsman of Roger de Hengham, a monk, and one of your brethren who was joined with me in that expedition to Rome, and was exposed to the same perils as myself, and in respect of the very same matter."

This said, we all rose and gave thanks; and Hugh, a clerk, brother of the said Roger, was nominated to the aforesaid church, saving to us our pension of ten marks.

CHAPTER VII
THE ABBOT AS PEER OF PARLIAMENT

IN that manor of the monks of Canterbury which is called Eleigh, and is within the hundred of the abbot, a case of homicide occurred; but the men of the archbishop would not permit that those manslayers should stand their trial in the court of St. Edmund. Thereupon the abbot made his plaint to King Henry, stating that Baldwin the archbishop was claiming for himself the liberties of our church, under authority of a new charter, which the King had given to the church of Canterbury after the death of St. Thomas. The King hereupon made answer, that he had never made any grant in derogation of the rights of our church, nor did he wish to take away from St. Edmund anything that had ever belonged to him.

On this intelligence, the abbot said to his most intimate advisers, "It is the better counsel that the archbishop should have to complain of me than I of the archbishop. I will put myself in seisin of this liberty, and afterwards will defend myself thereupon by the help of St. Edmund, whose right our charters testify it to be." Therefore suddenly and at daybreak, by the assistance of Robert of Cockfield, there were dispatched about fourscore men to the town of Eleigh, who took by surprise those three manslayers, and led them bound to St. Edmund, and cast them into the body of the gaol there.

Now, the archbishop complaining of this, Ranulf de Glanville, the justiciary, commanded that those men be put by gage and pledges to stand their trial in that court wherein they ought to stand trial; and the abbot was summoned to come before the King's court to answer touching the violence and injury which he was said to have done to the archbishop. The abbot thereupon offered himself several times without any essoin.

At length, upon Ash Wednesday, they stood before the King in the chapter house of Canterbury, and the charters of the King on one side and the other were read in court. And our lord the King said: "These charters are of the same age, and emanate from the same King, Edward. I know not what I can say, unless it be that these charters contradict each other." To whom the abbot said: "Whatever observations may apply to the charters, we are seised, and hitherto have been; and of this I am willing to put myself upon the verdict of the two counties of Norfolk and Suffolk, if they do allow this to be the case."

But Archbishop Baldwin, having first conferred with his advisers, said that the men of Norfolk and Suffolk greatly loved St. Edmund, and that great part of those counties was under the control of the abbot, and therefore he was unwilling to stand by their decision. The King at this waxed wroth, and in indignation got up, and in departing said, "He that is able to receive it, let him receive it." And so the matter was put off, and the case is yet undecided.

However, I observed that some of the men of the monks of Canterbury were wounded even to death by the country folk of the town of Milden, which is situate in the hundred of St. Edmund; and because they knew that the prosecutor ought to make suit to the jurisdiction wherein the culprit is, they chose to be silent and to put up with it, rather than make complaint thereupon to the abbot or his bailiffs, because in no wise would they come into the court of St. Edmund to plead there.

After this the men of Eleigh set up a certain cucking-stool, whereat justice was to be done in respect of deceits in the measuring of bread or corn; whereof the abbot complained to the Lord Bishop of Ely, then justiciary and chancellor. But he was anything but desirous to hear the abbot, because it was said that he was smelling after the archbishopric, which at that time was vacant. Some time afterwards, when he had come on a visitation, being entertained as legate, before he departed he made a speech at the shrine of the holy martyr. The abbot, seizing the opportunity, said to all present, "My lord bishop, the liberty which the monks of Canterbury claim for themselves is the right of St. Edmund, whose body is here present; and because you do not choose to render me assistance to protect the privileges of his church, I place that plaint between him and you. Let him from henceforth get justice done to himself." The chancellor deigned not to answer a single word; but within a year from that time was driven from England, and experienced divine vengeance.

Now when the same chancellor, on his return from Germany, had arrived at Ipswich, and rested the night at Hitcham, news was brought that he wished to take St. Edmund in his way, and would hear mass with us on the morrow. The abbot, therefore, gave strict injunctions that the offices of the church should not be celebrated so long as the chancellor was present in the church; for he said he had heard at London that the Bishop of London had pronounced in the presence of six bishops that the Chancellor was excommunicate, and had left England excommunicate, particularly for the violence he committed upon the Archbishop of York at Dover.

Therefore when the chancellor came to us on the morrow, he found no one, neither clerk nor monk, who would sing a mass. Indeed, not only the priest standing at the first mass, and beginning the canon of the mass, but the other priests standing before the altars, ceased, remaining with unmoved lips until a messenger came, saying that he had departed from the church. The chancellor put up with it at the time, but did many injuries to the abbot, until at length, by the intervention of friends, both parties returned to the kiss of peace.

When King Henry had taken the Cross, and had come to us within a month afterwards to pay his devotions, the abbot privily made for himself a cross of linen cloth, and holding in one hand the cross and a needle and thread, he requested licence from the King to take upon himself the cross. But this privilege was denied him, upon the suggestion of John, Bishop of Norwich, who said that it was not expedient for the country, or indeed safe for the counties of Norfolk and Suffolk, that the Bishop of Norwich and the Abbot of St. Edmund should be both away at the same time.

When the news came to London of the capture of King Richard and his imprisonment in Germany, and the barons met to take counsel thereupon, the abbot started up before them all, saying that he was quite ready to seek his lord the King, either in disguise or any other way, until he had discovered where he was, and had gained certain intelligence of him; by reason whereof he obtained great approbation.

When the chancellor, the Bishop of Ely, filled the office of legate, and in that capacity was holding a council at London, he proposed certain decrees against the black monks, taking notice of their wandering to St. Thomas and St. Edmund, on the excuse of pilgrimage, and inveighed against abbots, restricting them in the number of their horses. Abbot Samson replied, "We do not admit any decree against that rule of St. Benedict which allows the abbots the free and absolute government of their monks. I keep the barony of St. Edmund and his kingdom; nor are thirteen horses sufficient for me as they may be for some abbots, unless I have more to enable me to execute the King's justice."

Whilst there was war throughout England, during the captivity of King Richard, the abbot, with his whole convent, solemnly excommunicated all movers of the war and disturbers of the public peace, not fearing the Earl John, the King's brother, nor any other, so that he was styled the "stout-hearted abbot." After this he went to the siege of Windsor, where he appeared in armour with certain other abbots of England, having his own standard, and retaining many knights at heavy charges, being more remarkable there for his counsel than for his piety. But we cloister folk thought this act rather perilous, fearing lest in consequence some future abbot might be compelled to attend in person upon any warlike expedition. On the conclusion of a truce he went into Germany, and there visited the King with many gifts.

After the return of King Richard to England, licence was granted for holding tournaments; for which purpose many knights met between Thetford and St. Edmund. The abbot forbade them; but they, resisting, fulfilled their desire. On another occasion there came twenty-four young men with their followers, sons of noblemen, to have their revenge at the aforesaid place; which being done, they returned into the town to put up there. The abbot hearing of this, ordered the gates to be locked, and all of them to be kept within. The next day was the vigil of Peter and Paul the apostles. Therefore, having passed their word and promising that they would not go forth without permission, they all dined with the abbot on that day. After dinner, when the abbot retired to his chamber, they all arose and began to carol and sing, sending into the town for wine, drinking and then shouting, depriving the abbot and convent of their sleep, and doing everything in scorn of the abbot. They spent the day until the evening in this manner; and refused to desist, even when the abbot commanded them. But when evening was come, they broke open the gates of the town and went forth by force. The abbot, indeed, solemnly excommunicated all of them, yet not without first consulting Archbishop Hubert, at that time justiciary; and many of them came, promising amendment and seeking absolution.

The abbot often sent his messengers to Rome, by no means empty-handed. The first he sent, immediately after he was consecrated, obtained in general terms all the liberties and privileges which had been granted of yore to his predecessors, even in the time of the schism. Next he obtained, first among the abbots of England, that he might be able to give episcopal benediction solemnly, wheresoever he might happen to be, and this he obtained for himself and for his successors. Afterwards he obtained a general exemption for himself and his successors, from all Archbishops of Canterbury, which Abbot Hugh had only acquired for himself personally. In these confirmations Abbot Samson caused to be inserted many new privileges for the greater liberty and security of our church.

There once came a certain clerk to the abbot, bearing letters of request for procuring a benefice. And the abbot, drawing forth from his desk seven apostolic writings, with the leaden seals hanging to them, made answer: "Look at these apostolic writings, whereby divers popes require that certain benefices should be given to divers clerks. When I shall have quieted those who have come before you, I will give you your rent; for he who first cometh to the mill ought first to have his grist."

There was a general court summoned for the hundred of Risbridge, to hear the plaint and trial of the Earl of Clare, at Witham. He, indeed, accompanied by many barons and knights, including the Earl Alberic and many others, stated that his bailiffs had given him to understand that they were accustomed to receive yearly for his use five shillings from the hundred and the bailiffs of the hundred, and that this was now unjustly detained; and he alleged that the land of Alfric, the son of Withgar, who had in ancient time been lord of that hundred, had been granted to his predecessors at the conquest of England. But the abbot, taking thought for his own interest, without stirring from his place, answered, "It is a strange thing, my lord earl; your case fails you. King Edward the Confessor gave, and by his charter confirmed, to St. Edmund, this entire hundred; and of those five shillings there is no mention made therein. You must tell us for what service, or for what reason, you demand those five shillings." And the earl, after advising with his attendants, replied that it was his office to carry the standard of St. Edmund in battle, and for that cause the five shillings were due to him. The abbot answered, "Of a truth it seems a mean thing that such a man as the Earl of Clare, should receive such a petty gift for such a service. To the Abbot of St. Edmund, it is but a slight grievance to give five shillings. The Earl Roger Bigot holds himself as seised, and asserts that he is seised, of the office of bearing the standard of St. Edmund; indeed, he actually did bear it when the earl of Leicester was taken and the Flemings destroyed. Thomas of Mendham also claims this as his right. When, therefore, you shall have proved against these your right, I will with great pleasure pay you the five shillings you now seek to recover of me." The earl upon this said that he would talk the matter over with the Earl Roger, his kinsman, and so the matter was put off even to this day.

On the death of Robert of Cockfield, there came Adam, his son, and with him many of his relations, the Earl Roger Bigot, and many other great men, and made suit to the abbot for the tenements of the aforesaid Adam, and especially for the half hundred of Cosford, to be held by the annual payment of one hundred shillings, just as if it had been his hereditary right; indeed, they all said that his father and his grandfather had held it for fourscore years past and more.

When the abbot got an opportunity of speaking, putting his two fingers up to his two eyes, he said, "May I be deprived of these eyes on that day, nay, in that hour, wherein I grant to any one a hundred to be held in hereditary right, unless indeed the King, who is able to take away from me the abbey and my life with it, should force me to do so."

Explaining to them the reason of that saying, he averred, "If any one were to hold a hundred as an inheritance, and he should make forfeit to the King in any wise, so that he ought to lose his inheritance, forthwith will the Sheriff of Suffolk and the King's bailiffs have seisin of the hundred, and exercise their own power within our liberties; and if they should have the ward of the hundred, the liberty of the eight hundreds and a half will be endangered."

And then addressing himself to Adam, he said, "If you, who claim an inheritance in this hundred, should take to wife any free woman who should hold but one acre of land of the King in chief; the King, after your death, would possess himself of all that your tenement, together with the wardship of your son, if he be under age; and thus the King's bailiffs would enter upon the hundred of St. Edmund, to the prejudice of the abbot. Besides all this, your father acknowledged to me that he claimed nothing by right of inheritance in the hundred; but because his service was satisfactory to me, I permitted him to hold it all the days of his life, according as he deserved of me."

Upon the abbot saying thus much, money was offered; but he could not be persuaded by words or money. At last it was settled between them thus: Adam disclaimed the right which he had by word of mouth claimed in the hundred, and the abbot confirmed to him all his other lands; but touching our town of Cockfield, no mention was made of that, nor indeed is it believed that he had a charter thereof; Semer and Groton he was to hold for the term of his life.

Herbert the dean erected a windmill upon Haberdon. When the abbot heard of this, his anger was so kindled that he would scarcely eat or utter a single word. On the morrow, after hearing mass, he commanded the sacrist, that without delay he should send his carpenters thither and overturn it altogether, and carefully put by the wooden materials in safe keeping.

The dean, hearing this, came to him saying that he was able in law to do this upon his own frank fee, and that the benefit of the wind ought not to be denied to any one. He further said that he only wanted to grind his own corn there, and nobody else's, lest it should be imagined that he did this to the damage of the neighbouring mills. The abbot, his anger not yet appeased, answered, "I give you as many thanks as if you had cut off both my feet; by the mouth of God I will not eat bread until that building be plucked down. You are an old man, and you should have known that it is not lawful even for the King or his justiciary to alter or appoint a single thing within the banlieue, without the permission of the abbot and convent; and why have you presumed to do such a thing? Nor is this without prejudice to my mills, as you assert, because the burgesses will run to you and grind their corn at their pleasure, nor can I by law turn them away, because they are freemen. Nor would I endure that the mill of our cellarer, lately set up, should stand, except that it was erected before I was abbot. Begone," he said, "begone; before you have come to your house, you shall hear what has befallen your mill."

But the dean being afraid before the face of the abbot, by the counsel of his son, Master Stephen, forestalled the servants of the sacrist, and without delay caused that very mill which had been erected by his own servants to be overthrown. So that when the servants of the sacrist came thither, they found nothing to be pulled down.

The abbot was sued in respect of the advowson of certain churches, and gained the case. Certain others he also retained, although his right thereto was challenged, viz., the church of Westley, of Meringthorp, of Brettenham, of Wendling, of Pakenham, of Nowton, of Bradfield in Norfolk, the moiety of the church of Boxford, the church of Scaldwell, and the church of Endgate. All these, although the right was challenged by others, he retained, and he restored to his own right of patronage three portions of the church of Dickleburgh, and brought back the tenements belonging to those shares to the frank fee of the church, saving the service which was due therefrom to the manor of Tivetshall. But the church of Boxford being void, when an inquest was summoned thereupon, there came five knights tempting the abbot, and inquiring what it was they ought to swear.

The abbot would neither give nor promise to them anything, but said, "When the oath shall be administered, declare the right according to your consciences." They, indeed, being discontented, departed, and by their inquest took away from him the advowson of that church, namely, the last presentation. Nevertheless, he ultimately recovered it after many charges, and for a fine of ten marks.

The abbot also retained the church of Honington. This had not become vacant, but the right was challenged in the time of Durand of Hostesley, although he produced as evidence of his right the charter of William, Bishop of Norwich, wherein it was specified that Robert of Valognes, his father-in-law, had given that church to Ernald Lovell.

The moiety of the church of Hopton being void, a controversy arose thereupon between the abbot and Robert of Elm; and a day of hearing being appointed at Hopton, after much altercation, the abbot being guided by I know not what sudden impulse, said to the aforesaid Robert, "Do you but swear that this is your right, and I will allow that it shall be so." And since that knight refused to swear, it was by the consent of each party, referred to the oath of sixteen lawful men of the hundred, who swore that this belonged to the abbot as his right. Gilbert Fitz-Ralph and Robert of Cockfield, lords of that fee, were there present and consenting thereto.

Thereupon, Master Jordan de Ros, who had the charter of abbot Hugh, as well as the charter of the aforesaid Robert, starting forward, urged that whichever of them succeeded in proving his claim to the church, he (Jordan) might hold the parsonage, that he was parson of the whole church, and that the clerk last deceased had been his vicar, rendering him a yearly payment for that moiety. In proof thereof he produced the charter of Walchelin the archdeacon.

The abbot, greatly moved and angry with him, never received him in a friendly manner, until the said Jordan, in a chapter of the monks at Thetford, at the abbot's instance, resigned into the hands of the bishop there present that very moiety, without any reservation or expectation of afterwards recovering the same, before a great multitude of clerks. This done, the abbot said, "My lord bishop, I am engaged by promise to bestow the rent upon some one your clerk; and I now give this moiety of this church to whomsoever of your clerks you will." Then the bishop requested that in a friendly manner it should be given to the same Master Jordan; and so upon the presentation of the abbot, Jordan got it back again.

Afterwards a controversy arose between the abbot and the same Jordan, touching the land of Herard in Harlow, whether it were the frank fee of the church or not. And when there was summoned a jury of twelve knights to make inquest in the king's court, the inquest was taken in the court of the abbot at Harlow, by the licence of Ranulf de Glanville, and the recognitors swore that they never knew that land at any time to have been separated from the church, but nevertheless that land owed such service to the abbot as that to which the land of Eustace, and certain other lands of laymen in the same town were subject. At length it was agreed between them thus: Master Jordan in full court acknowledged that land to be lay fee, and that he claimed nothing therein, unless by the abbot's grace. He will therefore hold that land all the days of his life, rendering yearly to the abbot twelve pence for all services.

Since, according to the custom of the English, many persons gave many presents to the abbot, as being their head, upon the day of the Circumcision of our Lord, I, Jocelin, thought to myself, What can I give? And I began to reduce into writing all those churches which are in the gift of the abbot, as well of our manors as of his, and the reasonable values of the same, upon the same principle that they could be fairly set to farm, at a time when corn is at its ordinary standard price. And, therefore, upon the commencement of a new year, I gave to the abbot that schedule, as a gift to him, which he received very gratefully.

I, indeed, because I then was pleasing in his sight, thought in my heart, that I should hint to him that some one church should be given to the convent, and assigned for the purposes of hospitality, just as he had wished when he was a poor cloister monk: for this same thing he himself had, before his election, suggested the brethren should swear, that upon whomsoever the lot should fall, that man should do it. But while I thought upon these things, I remembered that some one previously had said the very same thing, and that I had heard the abbot reply, that he could not dismember the barony; in other words, that he ought not to diminish the liberty and dignity which abbot Hugh and others his predecessors had had, of giving away churches, which after all scarcely brought any gain or profit to the convent. On considering this, I held my peace.

The writing I have alluded to was the following:—

"These are the churches of the manors and socages of the ABBOT: The church of Melford is worth forty pounds; Chevington, ten marks; Saxham, twelve marks; Hargrave, five marks; Brettenham, five marks; Boxford, one hundred shillings; Fornham Magna, one hundred shillings; Stow, one hundred shillings; Honington, five marks; Elmswell, three marks; Cotton, twelve marks; Brocford, five marks; Palgrave, ten marks; Great Horningsherth, five marks; Kingston, four marks; Harlow, nineteen marks; Stapleford, three marks; Tivetshall, one hundred shillings; Worlingworth cum Bedingfield, twenty marks; Soham, six marks; the moiety of the church of Wortham, one hundred shillings; Rungton, twenty marks; Thorp, six marks; Woolpit, over and above the pension, one hundred shillings; Rushbrook, five marks; the moiety of the church of Hopton, sixty shillings; Rickinghall, six marks; three parts of the church of Dickleburgh, each part being worth thirty shillings and upwards; the moiety of the church of Gislingham, four marks; Icklingham, six marks. Concerning the church of Mildenhall, which is worth forty marks, and of the moiety of the church of Wetherden, what shall I say? Wendling, one hundred shillings; the church of Len, ten marks; the church of Scaldwell, five marks; the church of Warkton ...

"These are the churches of the manors belonging to the CONVENT: Mildenhall, Barton, and Horningsherth, twenty-five marks, besides the pension; Rougham, fifteen marks, besides the pension; Bradfield, five marks; Pakenham, thirty marks; Southrey, one hundred shillings; Risby, twenty marks; Nowton, four marks; Whepstead, fourteen marks; Fornham St. Genevieve, fifteen marks; Herringswell, nine marks; Fornham St. Martin, three marks; Ingham, ten marks; Lackford, one hundred shillings; Elveden, ten marks; Cockfield, twenty marks; Semer-Semer, twelve marks; Groton, five marks; the moiety of the church of Fressingfield, fourteen marks; Beccles, twenty marks; Broc, fifteen marks; Hinderclay, ten marks; Warkton, ten marks; Scaldwell, five marks; Westley, five marks; the church in Norwich, two marks, over and above the payment of herrings; and two churches in Colchester, three marks, over and above the pension of four shillings; Chelsworth, one hundred shillings; Meringthorp, four marks; the moiety of the church of Bradfield in Norfolk, three marks; staffacres and fouracres, and the third part of the tithes of the lordships of Wrabness, six marks."

The two counties of Norfolk and Suffolk were put in the "mercy" of the King by the justices in eyre for some default, and fifty marks were put upon Norfolk, and thirty upon Suffolk. And when a certain portion of that common amerciament was assessed upon the lands of St. Edmund, and was sharply demanded, the abbot, without any delay, went to our lord the King. We found him at Clarendon; and when the charter of King Edward, which discharges all the lands of St. Edmund from all gelds and scots, had been shown to him, the King commanded by his writ that six knights of the county of Norfolk and six of Suffolk should be summoned to consider before the barons of the exchequer, whether the lordships of St. Edmund ought to be quit from common amerciament. To save trouble and expense, only six knights were chosen, and these for the reason that they had lands in either county; namely, Hubert of Briseword, W. Fitz-Hervey, and William of Francheville, and three others, who went to London with us, and on behalf of the two counties gave their verdict in favour of the liberty of our church. And thereupon the justices then sitting enrolled their verdict.

The abbot Samson entered into a contest with his knights—himself against all, and all of them against him. He had stated to them that they ought to perform the service of fifty individual knights in escuages, in aids, and the like, because, as they themselves said, they held so many knights' fees. The point in dispute was, why ten of those fifty knights were to be without performing service, or by what reason or by whose authority the forty should receive the help of those ten knights. But they all answered with one voice, that such had ever been the custom, that is to say, that ten of them should assist the other forty, and that they could not thereupon—nor ought they thereupon—to answer, nor yet to implead.

When they were summoned in the King's court to answer hereupon, some, by arrangement, excused themselves from appearing, the others cunningly appeared, saying that they ought not to answer without their peers. On another occasion, those presented themselves who had first absented themselves, saying in like manner, that they ought not to answer without their peers who were joined with them in the same plaint. And when they had several times thus mocked the abbot, and had involved him in great and grievous expenses, the abbot complained of this to Hubert, the archbishop, then justiciary, who replied in open court that each knight ought to plead singly, and in respect of his own tenure, and said straight out that the abbot was clever enough and able enough to prove the rights of his church against all and every one of them. Then the earl, Roger Bigot, first of all freely confessed that, in law, he owed to his superior lord the abbot his service of three entire knights' fees, in reliefs as well as in escuages and aids; but, so far as concerned his performing castle-guard at the castle of Norwich, he said nothing.

Next came two of these knights, then three, and again more, until nearly all of them had come, and, by the earl's example, acknowledged the same service. Because such acknowledgment thereupon made in the court of St. Edmund was not sufficient in law, the abbot took all of them to London at his own charges, with the wives and women who were inherited of the lands so held, that they should make the acknowledgment in the King's court, and they all received separate charters of the concord thus made. Alberic de Vere and William of Hastings and two others were in the King's service beyond sea when this was done, and therefore the plaint concerning them was stayed. Alberic de Vere was the last who held out against the abbot; but as it was, the abbot seized and sold his cattle, wherefore it behoved him to come into court, and answer, as did his fellows. Taking advice upon it, he at length acknowledged to the abbot and St. Edmund their right.

The knights, therefore, being all defeated, a great profit would have accrued to the abbot from this victory unless he had been inclined to spare some of them; for so often as twenty shillings are charged upon a fee, there will remain twelve pounds to the abbot, and if more or less are assessed, more or less will remain over as a surplus to him, according to the strict apportionment. Also the abbot was wont, as were his predecessors, at the end of every twenty weeks to give seven shillings for the guard of the castle of Norwich out of his own purse, for default of three knights, whose fees Roger Bigot holds of St. Edmund. Each of the knights of four constabularies used to give twenty-eight pence when they entered to perform their guards, and one penny to the marshal who collected those pence; and they were accustomed to give twenty-eight pence and no more, because the ten knights of the fifth constabulary ought to assist the other forty, so that whereas they ought to have given three shillings entire, they only gave twenty-nine pence, and he whose duty it was to enter to perform his guard service at the end of four months, entered at the end of twenty weeks. But at the present time all the knights give the full three shillings, and there remains to the abbot the surplus which accrues beyond twenty-nine pence, from whence he can re-imburse himself of the aforesaid seven shillings. It is apparent what force had the words of the abbot which he spoke the first day, when he took the homage of his knights, as aforesaid, when all the knights promised him twenty shillings, and immediately revoked what they had said, refusing to give him more than forty pounds in one sum, alleging that ten knights ought to assist the other forty in aids and castle-guards, and all such like services.

There is certain land in Tivetshall of the abbot's fee, which used to pay to the watchmen of the castle of Norwich waite-fee, that is, twenty shillings per annum, payable five shillings on each of the four Ember fasts. This is an ancient customary payment which the abbot would well wish to do away with if he could, but considering his inability to do so, he has up to now held his peace and closed his eyes to it.

CHAPTER VIII
THE CASE OF HENRY OF ESSEX

[FOR the purpose of diffusing the knowledge of the blessed King and martyr, we have annexed this, we hope not irrelevantly, to the foregoing. Not that I who am so insignificant a person, and of scarcely any account, should set it forth with a historical title; but insomuch as Master Jocelin, our almoner, a man of exalted piety, powerful in word and deed, did so begin it at the request and desire of his superior, I may look upon it as my own work, because, according to the precept of Seneca, whatever has been well said by another, I may without presumption ascribe to myself.

When the abbot came to Reading, and we with him, we were suitably entertained by the monks of that place, among whom we met Henry of Essex, a professed monk, who, having obtained an opportunity of speaking with the abbot, related to him and ourselves as we all sat together, how he was vanquished in duel, and how and for what reason St. Edmund had confounded him in the very hour of battle. I therefore reduced his tale into writing by the command of the lord abbot, and wrote it in these words.

As it is impossible for us to shun evil unless it be apparent, we have thought it worthy to commit to historical record the acts and excesses of Henry of Essex, as a warning and not for imitation. The warnings that can be enforced by anecdotes are useful and beneficial. The aforesaid Henry, therefore, while in prosperity was in high esteem amongst the great men of the realm, a man of much account, of noble birth, conspicuous by deeds of arms, the king's standard-bearer, and feared by all on account of his power. His neighbours endowed the church of St. Edmund, the King and martyr, with possessions and rents; but he not only shut his eyes to this fact, but also by force and by injuries, with violence and evil speaking, wrongfully withheld an annual rent of five shillings, and converted it to his own use. Nay, indeed, in process of time, when a cause touching the rape of a certain damsel was prosecuted in the court of St. Edmund, the said Henry came thither, protesting and alleging that the same plaint by law ought to be decided in his court, in view of the birthplace of the same damsel, who was born within his lordship of Lailand; and by reason of this pretext he presumed to harass the court of St. Edmund with journeys and innumerable expenses for a long space of time.

In the meantime, in these and such like acts, fortune, smiling upon his desires, suddenly brought in upon him the cause of perpetual sorrow, and, under the appearance of a joyful beginning, she contrived for him a joyless end; for she is wont to smile that she may afterwards rage, to flatter that she may deceive, to raise up that she may cast down. All at once, there rose up against him Robert of Montfort, his kinsman and equal in birth and power, impeaching and accusing him before the princes of the land, of treason against the King. For he asserted that Henry, in the war with the Welsh, in the difficult pass of Coleshill, had traitorously thrown down the standard of our lord the King, and had with a loud voice proclaimed his death, and so turned to flight those who were hastening to his assistance. In point of fact, the aforesaid Henry of Essex did believe that the famous King Henry the Second, who had been intercepted by the stratagems of the Welsh, had been killed; and this would indeed have been the case, if Roger Earl of Clare, illustrious (clarus) by reason of birth, and more illustrious by deeds of valour, had not come up in good time with his Clare men, and raised the standard of our lord the King, to the encouragement and heartening of the whole army. Henry, indeed, strenuously opposed the aforesaid Robert in a speech, and absolutely denied the accusation, so that after a short lapse of time it came to a trial by battle. And they came to Reading to fight in a certain island hard by the abbey; and thither also came a multitude to see what issue the matter would take.

Now it came to pass, while Robert of Montfort thundered upon him manfully with hard and frequent strokes, and a bold onset had promised the fruit of victory, Henry, his strength a little failing him, glanced round on all sides, and lo! on the border of the land and water he saw the glorious King and martyr, Edmund, armed, and as if hovering in the air, looking towards him with a severe countenance, shaking his head with threats of anger and indignation. He also saw with him another knight, Gilbert of Cereville, not only in appearance inferior, but less in stature from the shoulders, direct his eyes upon him as if angry and wrathful. This man, by the order of the same Henry, had been afflicted with chains and torments, and had closed his days in prison at the instance and on the accusation of Henry's wife; who, turning her own wickedness upon an innocent person, stated that she could not endure the solicitations of Gilbert to unlawful love. Therefore, Henry, on sight of these apparitions, became anxious and fear-stricken, and remembered that old crime brings new shame. Becoming wholly desperate, and changing reason into violence, he assumed the part of one who attacked, not one who was on the defensive; who, while he struck fiercely, was more fiercely struck; and while he manfully fought, was more manfully attacked in his turn. In short, he fell vanquished.

As he was believed to be dead, upon the petition of the great men of England, his kinsmen, it was permitted that the monks of that place should give his body the rites of sepulture. Nevertheless, he afterwards recovered, and now with restored health, he has wiped out the blot upon his previous life under the regular habit, and in his endeavour to cleanse the long week of his dissolute life by at least one purifying sabbath, has so cultivated the studies of the virtues, as to bring forth the fruit of happiness.]

CHAPTER IX
TROUBLES WITHOUT

GEOFFREY Ridel, Bishop of Ely, sought from the abbot some timber for the purpose of constructing certain great buildings at Glemsford. This request the abbot granted, but against his will, not daring to offend him. Now the abbot making some stay at Melford, there came a certain clerk of the bishop, asking on behalf of his lord, that the promised timber might be taken at Elmswell; and he made a mistake in the word, saying Elmswell when he should have said Elmsett, which is the name of a certain wood at Melford. And the abbot was astonished at the request, for such timber was not to be found at Elmswell.

Now when Richard the forester of the same town had heard of this, he secretly informed the abbot that the bishop had the previous week sent his carpenters to spy out the wood of Elmsett, and had chosen the best timber trees in the whole wood, and placed his marks thereon. On hearing this, the abbot directly discovered that the messenger of the bishop had made an error in his request, and answered that he would willingly do as the bishop pleased.

On the morrow, upon the departure of the messenger, immediately after he had heard mass, the abbot went into the before-named wood with his carpenters, and caused to be branded with his mark not only all the oaks previously marked, but more than a hundred others, for the use of St. Edmund, and for the steeple of the great tower, commanding that they should be felled as quickly as possible. When the bishop, by the answer of his messenger, understood that the aforesaid timber might be taken at Elmswell, he sent back the same messenger (whom he overwhelmed with many hard words) to the abbot, in order that he might correct the word which he had mistaken, by saying Elmsett, not Elmswell. But before he had come to the abbot, all the trees which the bishop desired and his carpenters had marked were felled. So the bishop, if he wanted timber, had to get other timber elsewhere. As for myself, when I witnessed this affair, I laughed, and said in my heart, "Thus art is deceived by art."

On the death of Abbot Hugh, the wardens of the abbey desired to depose the bailiffs of the town of St. Edmund, and to appoint new bailiffs of their own authority, saying that this appertained to the King, in whose hand the abbey then was. But we, complaining thereof, sent our messengers to lord Ranulf de Glanville, then justiciary. He answered, that he well knew that forty pounds a year ought to be paid from the town to our sacrist, specially for the lights of the church; and he said that Abbot Hugh, of his own will, and in his privy chamber, without the consent of the convent, had granted the bailiwick as often as he chose, and unto whom he chose, saving the forty pounds payable to the altar. And therefore it was not to be wondered at if the King's bailiffs required this same thing on the King's behalf. Speaking in bitter language, he called all our monks fools for having permitted our abbot to do such things, not considering that the chief duty of monks is to hold their peace, and pass over with closed eyes the excesses of their prelates; nor yet considering that they are called barrators if they, whether it be right or wrong, contravene their superiors in anything; and, further, that sometimes we are accused of treason and are condemned to prison and to exile. Wherefore it seems to myself and others the better counsel to die as confessors rather than as martyrs.

On the return of our messenger home, and on his relating what he had seen and heard, we, as being unwilling and, as it were, under compulsion, resolved, so far as we were able, that the old bailiffs of the town should be deposed, as well with the common consent of the convent, as by the keepers of the abbey. Samson, then sub-sacrist, was very reluctant to join in this proposition. However, when Samson was made abbot, he, calling to remembrance the wrong done to the abbey, on the morrow after the Easter following his election, caused to be assembled in our chapter-house the knights and clerks, and a number of the burgesses, and then in the presence of them all, said that the town belonged to the convent and to the altar, namely, to find tapers for the church; and that he was desirous of renewing the ancient custom, so that in the presence of the convent, and with the consent of all, some measure should be taken concerning the bailiwick of the town, and of such like matters which appertained to the convent.

At that time were nominated two burgesses, Godfrey and Nicholas, to be bailiffs; and a discussion taking place from whose hand they should receive the horn, which is called the moot-horn, at last they took it from the hands of the prior, who, next to the abbot, is head over the affairs of the convent.

Now these two bailiffs kept their bailiwick in peace many years, until they were said to be remiss in keeping the King's justice. On the abbot's suggestion that greater security should be given to the convent upon this point, they were removed, and Hugh the sacrist took the town into his own keeping, appointing new officers, who were to answer to him concerning the bailiwick. In process of time, I know not how, new bailiffs were subsequently appointed, and that elsewhere than in chapter, and without the concurrence of the church; wherefore a like or perhaps greater peril is to be apprehended after the decease of Abbot Samson than even was after the death of Abbot Hugh.

One of our brethren, too, fully relying upon the regard and friendship of the abbot, upon a fit opportunity and with propriety and decency, talked over the matter with him, asserting that dissatisfaction was expressed in the convent. But the abbot upon hearing this was silent for a long time, as if he was somewhat disturbed. At length he is reported to have said, "Am not I, even I, the abbot? Does it not belong to me alone to make order concerning the affairs of the church committed to my care, provided only that I should act with wisdom and according to God's will? If there should be default in the administration of the King's justice in this town, I shall be challenged for it; I shall be summoned; upon myself alone will rest the burden of the journey, and the expenses, and the defence of the town and its appurtenances; I alone shall be deemed a fool, not the prior, not the sacrist, nor yet the convent, but myself, who am and ought to be their head. Through me and my counsel, with God's assistance, will the town be securely preserved to the best of my ability, and safe also will be those forty pounds payable annually to the altar. Let the brethren grumble, let them slander me, let them say amongst themselves what they will, I am still their father and their abbot; so long as I live 'I will not give my glory to another.'" This said, that monk departed, and reported these answers to us.

I for my part marvelled at such sayings, and argued with myself in various ways. At length I was compelled to remain in a state of doubt, inasmuch as the rule of law says and teaches, that all things should be under the governance of the abbot.

The merchants of London claimed to be quit of toll at the fair of St. Edmund. Nevertheless many paid it, unwillingly indeed, and under compulsion; whereof a great tumult and commotion was made among the citizens in London at their hustings. They came in a body and informed Abbot Samson that they were entitled to be quit of toll throughout all England, by authority of the charter which they had from King Henry the Second. The abbot answered that were it necessary, he was well able to vouch the King to warrant that he had never granted them any charter to the prejudice of our church, or to the prejudice of the liberties of St. Edmund, to whom St. Edward had granted and confirmed toll and theam and all regalities before the conquest of England; and that King Henry had done no more than give to the Londoners an exemption from toll throughout his own lordships, and in places where he was able to grant it; but so far as concerned the town of St. Edmund he was not able so to do, for it was not his to dispose of. The Londoners, hearing this, ordered by common council that none of them should go to the fair of St. Edmund. For two years they kept away, whereby our fair sustained great loss, and the offering of the sacrist was much diminished. At last, upon the mediation of the Bishop of London and many others, it was settled between us and them that they should come to the fair, and that some of them should pay toll, but that it should be forthwith returned to them, that by such a colourable act the privilege on both sides should be preserved.

But in process of time, when the abbot had made agreement with his knights, and as it were slept in tranquillity, behold again "the Philistines be upon thee, Samson!" Lo! the Londoners, with one voice, were threatening that they would lay level with the earth the stone houses which the abbot had built that very year, or that they would take distress by a hundredfold from the men of St. Edmund, unless the abbot forthwith redressed the wrong done them by the bailiffs of the town of St. Edmund, who had taken fifteen pence from the carts of the citizens of London, who in their way from Yarmouth, laden with herrings, had made passage through our demesnes. Furthermore, the citizens of London said that they were quit of toll in every market, and on every occasion, and in every place throughout all England, from the time when Rome was first founded, and that London was founded at the very same time. Also, that they ought to have such an exemption throughout all England, as well by reason of its being a privileged city, which was of old time the metropolis and head of the kingdom, as by reason of its antiquity. The abbot asked that the matter might be deferred until the return of our lord the King to England, that he might consult with him upon this; and having taken advice of the lawyers, he replevied to the claimants those fifteen pence, without prejudice to the question of each party's right.

In the tenth year of the abbacy of Abbot Samson, by the common counsel of our chapter, we complained to the abbot in his own hall, stating that the rents and issues of all the good towns and boroughs of England were increasing and augmenting, to the profit of the possessors, and the well-thriving of their lords, all except this our town, which had long yielded forty pounds, and had never gone beyond that sum; and that the burgesses of the town were the cause of this thing. For they held so large and so many standings in the market-place, of shops and sheds and stalls, without the assent of the convent, indeed from the sole gift of the bailiffs of the town, who in old time were but yearly renters, and, as it were, ministers of the sacrist, and were removable at his good pleasure. The burgesses, being summoned, made answer that they were under the jurisdiction of the King's courts, nor would they make answer in derogation of the immunity of the town and their charters, in respect of the tenements which they and their fathers had holden well and peaceably for one year and a day without claim. They also said the old custom had been that the bailiffs should, without the interference of the convent, dispose of the places of the shops and sheds in the market-place, in consideration of a certain rent payable yearly to the bailiwick. But we, gainsaying this, were desirous that the abbot should disseise them of tenements for which they had no warranty.

Now the abbot coming to our council, as if he were one of us, said to us in private, that he was willing enough to do us right, according to the best of his ability, but that he, nevertheless, was bound to proceed in due course of law; nor could he, without the judgment of a court, disseise his free men of their lands or rents, which they had held for many years, were it justly or unjustly. If he should do this, he said, he should fall into the King's mercy by the assize of the realm. Therefore, the burgesses, taking counsel together, offered to the convent a rent of one hundred shillings for the sake of peace; and that they should hold their tenements as they had been wont to do. But we, on the other hand, were by no means willing to grant this, rather desiring to put that plaint in respite, hoping, perhaps, in the time of another abbot, to recover all, or change the place of the fair; and so the affair was deferred for many years.

When the abbot had returned from Germany, the burgesses offered him sixty marks, and sued for his confirmation of the liberties of the town, under the same form of words as Anselm, and Ording, and Hugh had confirmed them; all which the abbot graciously accorded. Notwithstanding our murmuring and grumbling, a charter was accordingly made to them in the terms of his promise; and because it would have been a shame and confusion to him if he had not been able to fulfil his promise, we were not willing to contradict him, or provoke him to anger.

The burgesses, indeed, from the period when they had the charter of Abbot Samson and the convent, became more confident that they, at least in the time of Abbot Samson, would not lose their tenements or their franchises; so that never afterwards, as they did before, were they willing to pay or offer the before-named rent of one hundred shillings. At length, however, the abbot giving attention to this matter, discoursed with the burgesses hereupon, saying that unless they made their peace with the convent, he should forbid their erecting their booths at the fair of St. Edmund.

They, on the other hand, answered that they were willing to give every year a silken cope, or some other ornament, to the value of one hundred shillings, as they had before promised to do; but nevertheless, upon this condition, that they were to be for ever quit of the tithes of their profits, which the sacrist sharply demanded of them. The abbot and the sacrist both refused this, and therefore the plaint was again put in respite.

In point of fact, we have from that time to the present lost those hundred shillings, according to the old saying, "He that will not when he may, when he will he shall have nay."

CHAPTER X
TROUBLES WITHIN

THE cellarers quickly succeeded each other, and every one of them at the year's end became involved in a great debt. There were given to the cellarer, in aid, twenty pounds out of Mildenhall, but this did not suffice. After that, fifty pounds were assigned to the cellarer each year from the same manor; and yet the cellarer used to say that this was not enough. The abbot, therefore, being anxious to provide for his security from loss and comfort, as well as for our own, knowing that in all our wants we must have recourse to him as to the father of the monastery, associated with the cellarer a certain clerk of his own table, by name Ranulf, so that he might assist him both as a witness and companion in the expenses and receipts. And lo! many of us speak many things, murmurings thicken, falsehoods are invented, scandals are interwoven with scandals, nor is there a corner in the house which does not resound with venomous hissing.

One says to another, "What is this that is done? Who ever saw the like? There never was such an insult offered to the convent before. Behold! the abbot has set a clerk over a monk; see, he has made a clerk a master and keeper over the cellarer, as if he could do no good without him. The abbot thinks but lightly of his monks; he suspects his monks; he consults clerks; he loves clerks. 'How is the gold become dim! How is the fine gold changed!'" Also one friend says to another, "We are become a reproach to our neighbours. All of us monks are either reckoned faithless or improvident; the clerk is believed, the monk is not. The abbot had rather trust the clerk than the monk. Now is this clerk a whit more faithful or wise than a monk would be?"

And again, one friend would say to another, "Are not the cellarer and sub-cellarer, or can they not be, as faithful as the sacrist or the chamberlain? The consequence is, that this abbot or his successor will put a clerk along with the sacrist, a clerk with the chamberlain, a clerk with the sub-sacrists to collect the offerings at the shrine, and so on with all the officials, wherefore we shall be a laughing-stock and derision to the whole people."

I, hearing these things, was accustomed to answer, "If I, for my part, were cellarer, I had rather that a clerk were a witness for me in all my transactions; for if I did well he would bear witness of the good. If, again, I had, at the end of the year, become laden with debt, I should be able to gain credence and to be excused by the testimony of that clerk."

I heard, indeed, one of our brethren, a man truly discreet and learned, say something upon this subject which struck myself and others very much. "It is not," he said, "to be wondered at, should the lord abbot interpose his exertions in the safe conduct of our affairs, especially as he wisely manages that portion of the abbey which belongs to him, and is discreet in the disposing of his own house, it being his part to supply our wants in case of our carelessness or inability to do so. But there is one thing," he added, "which will prove dangerous after the death of the abbot Samson, such as has never come to pass in our days or in our lives. Of a surety the King's bailiffs will come, and will possess themselves of the abbey, I mean the barony which belongs to the abbot, as was done in the past after the deaths of other Abbots. As after the death of Abbot Hugh, the King's bailiffs likewise desired to appoint new bailiffs in the town of St. Edmund, alleging as their warrant that Abbot Hugh had done this, in the same way the King's bailiffs will, in process of time, appoint their clerk to keep the cellary, in order that everything shall be done therein by him, and under his discretion. And then we shall be told that they are entitled to act in this manner because Abbot Samson did so. Thus they will have the power of intermixing and confusing all the concerns and rents of the abbot and of the convent; all which, indeed, Abbot Robert, of good memory, had, with due consideration, distinguished in account, and had separated one from the other."

When I heard these and such like expressions from a man of great thought and foresight, I was astonished, and held my peace, not wishing either to condemn the lord abbot, or to excuse him.

Hubert Walter, the Archbishop of Canterbury and legate of the apostolic see, and Justiciary of England, after he had visited many churches, and had by right of his legation made many changes and alterations, was on his way home from his natural mother, who lived at Dereham and was then dying. He sent two of his clerks over to us, bearing the sealed letters of their lord, wherein it was contained that we should give credit to what they should say and do. These men inquired of the abbot and convent whether we were willing to receive their lord, the legate, who was on his way to us, in such wise as a legate ought to be received, and, in fact, is received by other churches. If we were agreed to this, he would shortly come to us, for the purpose of making order concerning the matters and affairs of our church according to God's will; but if we were not agreed, those two clerks could more fully communicate to us their lord's behest. Thereupon the abbot called together most of the convent, and we came to the decision that we would give a gracious answer to the clerks thus sent to us, saying that we were willing to receive their lord as legate with all honour and reverence, and to send together with them our own messengers, who, on our part, should communicate the same to the lord legate.

Our intention was that, in the same way as we had done to the Bishop of Ely and other legates, we would show him all possible honour, with a procession and ringing of bells, and would receive him with the usual solemnities, until it should come to the point, perhaps, of his holding a visitation in chapter. If he were to proceed in doing this, then all of us were to oppose him might and main to his face, appealing to Rome, and standing upon our charters. And the lord abbot said, "If at this present time the legate will come to us, we will do as is aforesaid, but if indeed he shall defer his arrival to us for a time, we will consult the lord Pope, and inquire what force the privileges of our church ought to have, as being those which have been obtained from him and his predecessors, against the archbishop who has now obtained power from the apostolic see over all the privileged churches of England." Such was our determination.

When the archbishop had heard that we were willing to receive him as legate, he received our messengers graciously and with giving of thanks. And he became favourable and kindly disposed towards the lord abbot in all his concerns, and for certain pressing causes deferred his visit to us for a time. Therefore, without the least delay, the abbot sent to the Pope the same letters which the legate had sent to him and the convent, wherein it was contained that he was about to come to us by authority of his legation, and by the authority of the Pope, and, moreover, that to him was given power over all the exempt churches of England, notwithstanding the letters of exemption obtained by the church of York or any other.

The abbot's messenger expediting the matter, our lord the Pope wrote to the lord of Canterbury, asserting that our church, as his spiritual daughter, ought not to be accountable to any legate, unless he were a legate of our lord the Pope sent *a latere*, and enjoined him that he should not stretch forth his hand against us; and our lord the Pope added as from himself a prohibition against his exercising jurisdiction over any other exempt church. Our messenger returned to us, and this was kept a secret for many days. Nevertheless, the same was intimated to the lord of Canterbury by some of his adherents at the court of our lord the Pope.

When, at the end of the year, the legate made his visitation through Norfolk and Suffolk, and had first arrived at Colchester, the legate sent his messenger to the abbot, privately letting him thereby know that he (the legate) had heard say that the abbot had obtained letters contravening his legation, and requesting that he, in a friendly way, would send him those letters. And it was done accordingly, for the abbot had two counterparts of these letters. The abbot, indeed, did not pay a visit to the legate, either by himself or by proxy, so long as he was in the diocese of Norwich, lest it should be thought that he wished to make fine with the legate for his entertainment, as other monks and canons had done. The legate, disconcerted and angry and fearing to be shut out if he came to us, passed by Norwich, by Acre and by Dereham to Ely, on his way to London.

The abbot meeting the legate within the month, between Waltham and London, on the King's highway, the legate censured him for having refused to meet him, as being justiciary of our lord the King whilst he was in that country. The abbot answered that he had not travelled as justiciary, but as legate, making visitation in every church; and alleged the reason of the time of year, and that the passion of our Lord was nigh at hand, and that it behoved him to be concerned with Divine services and cloister duties.

When the abbot had opposed words to words, and objections to objections, and could neither be bent nor intimidated by threatening language, the legate replied with scorn that he well knew him to be a keen wrangler, and that he was a better clerk than he, the legate, was. The abbot, therefore, not timidly passing by matters inexpedient to allude to, nor yet arrogantly speaking upon matters that were to be discussed, in the hearing of many persons made answer that he was a man who would never suffer the privileges of his church to be shaken either for want of learning or money, even if it should come to pass that he lost his life, or was condemned to perpetual banishment. However, these and other altercations being brought to a close, the legate began to flush in the face, upon the abbot lowering his tone and beseeching him that he would deal more gently with the church of St. Edmund, by reason of his native soil, for he was native born of St. Edmund, and had been his fosterling. And, indeed, he had reason to blush, because he had so unadvisedly outpoured the venom which he had bred within him.

On the morrow it was communicated to the Archbishop of Canterbury, that the lord Archbishop of York was about to come as legate into England, and that he had suggested many evil things to the Pope concerning him, stating that he had oppressed the churches of England by reason of his visitation to the extent of thirty thousand marks, which he had received from them. The legate, therefore, sent his clerks to the abbot, begging him that he would, with the other abbots, write to our lord the Pope and justify him.

This the abbot willingly did, and thereby offered his testimony that the lord of Canterbury had not been to our church, nor had he oppressed any other church, speaking according to his conscience. And when the abbot had delivered those letters to the messengers of the archbishop, he said before us all that he did not fear, even if it were the archbishop's wish to deal deceitfully with those letters. The clerks answered on the peril of their souls, that their lord did not contemplate any subtle dealings, but only wished to be justified. And so the archbishop and the abbot were made friends.

CHAPTER XI
SAMSON'S CONTESTS WITH KNIGHTS, MONKS AND TOWNSMEN

KING Richard commanded all the bishops and abbots of England that for every nine knights of their baronies they should make a tenth knight, and that without delay those knights should go to him in Normandy, with horses and arms, in aid against the King of France. Wherefore it behoved the abbot to account to him for sending four knights. And when he had caused to be summoned all his knights, and had conferred with them thereon, they made answer that their fees, which they had holden of St. Edmund, were not liable to this charge, neither had they or their fathers ever gone out of England, although they had, on some occasions, paid escuage by the King's writ.

The abbot was indeed in a strait; on one hand observing that hereby the liberty of his knights was in peril, on the other hand apprehending that he might lose the seisin of his barony for default in the King's service, as indeed had befallen the Bishop of London and many English barons. So he forthwith went beyond seas to the King; and though fatigued with many troubles and expenses, and very many presents which he gave the King, in the first instance he could make no agreement with the King by money. For the King said that he did not want either silver or gold, but that he instantly required four knights; whereupon the abbot obtained four mercenaries. When the King had got these, he sent them to the Castle of Eu, and the abbot paid them thirty-six marks down for their expenses for forty days.

Now on the morrow, there came certain of the King's attendants, and recommended the abbot to carefully look to what he was about, stating that the war might possibly last a whole year or more, and that the expenses of the knights would consequently increase and multiply, to the endless damage of him and his church. They therefore advised him that before he left the court he should make fine with the King, so that he might be quit in respect of the service of the aforesaid knights after the forty days were passed. The abbot, having adopted this good counsel, gave to the King one hundred pounds for such a quittance. Thus being in favour with his sovereign, he returned to England, bringing with him the King's writ, commanding that his knights should be distrained by their fees to render him that King's service which he had got performed for them.

The knights, being summoned, alleged their poverty and manifold grievances, and prevailed upon their lord to accept two marks upon every shield. The abbot, indeed, not forgetting that he had that same year burdened them much, and had impleaded them to make them render their escuage individually, was desirous of conciliating their esteem, and in good part accepted what they with a good grace offered.

At that time, although the abbot had been put to great expenses beyond sea, yet he did not return home to this church empty-handed; for he brought with him a golden cross, and a most valuable copy of the Gospels, of the value of fourscore marks. On another occasion when he returned from beyond seas, sitting in chapter, he said that if he had been cellarer or chamberlain he would have made some purchase which would have been serviceable to his office; and since he was abbot, he ought to purchase something that should beseem him as abbot. After saying this, he offered to the convent a valuable chasuble, and a mitre interwoven with gold, and sandals with silken buskins, and the head of a crozier of silver and well wrought. In like manner, so often as he returned from beyond sea, he brought along with him some ornament or other.

In the year of grace one thousand one hundred and ninety-seven, certain innovations and alterations took place in our church, which ought not to be passed over in silence. Insomuch as his ancient rents were not sufficient for our cellarer, Abbot Samson ordered that fifty pounds from Mildenhall should be given by way of increase to the cellarer yearly by the hands of the prior, not all at one time, but by monthly instalments, so that he should have something every month to expend, and that it should not all be disbursed at one time of the year.

And so it was done for one year. But the cellarer with his fellows complained of this, saying that if he had that money in hand, he would provide himself and preserve a sufficient stock. The abbot, although unwillingly, granted his petition. Now, on the commencement of the month of August, the cellarer had already spent all, and, moreover, was in debt twenty pounds, and a debt of fifty pounds was about to fall due before Michaelmas.

Hearing of this, the abbot was wroth, and thus spoke in chapter: "I have often and often threatened that I will take the cellarership into my own hands on account of your default and improvidence, for all of you keep incumbering yourselves with heavy debts. I put my own clerk with your cellarer as a witness, and in order that matters should be more advisedly managed; but there is neither clerk nor monk who dares to inform me of the real cause of debt. It is nevertheless said that excess of feasting in the prior's house, by the assent of the prior and cellarer, and superfluous expenses in the guest-house by the carelessness of the hospitaller, are the cause of all this. You see," he continued, "what a great debt is now pressing; give me your advice, and tell me how this matter can be amended."

Many of the cloister folk hearing this, and half smiling, took what was said in very good part, saying privily, "All that the abbot says is true enough." The prior cast the blame upon the cellarer, the cellarer in his turn upon the hospitaller; each one justified himself. We all of us well knew the truth of the matter, but we held our tongues, for we were afraid. On the morrow came the abbot, and said again to the convent: "Give me your opinion as to the means whereby your cellar can be better and more economically managed." But there was no one who answered, except one, who said that there was no superfluity at all in the refectory which could occasion such a debt or pressure. On the third day the abbot spoke the same words, and one answered, "That advice ought to proceed from yourself, as from our head."

Then the abbot said, "As you will not state your opinion, and as you are incapable of managing your house for yourselves, the management of the monastery rests solely upon myself as father and supreme keeper. I take," he said, "into my own hand your cellar and the charge of the guests, and the stewardship of everything indoors and out of doors." So saying he deposed the cellarer and hospitaller, and put in their stead two other monks, under the style of sub-cellarer and hospitaller, associating with them Master G., a clerk of his own table, without whose assent nothing could be done, either in respect of meat or drink, or in regard to disbursements or receipts.

The old purveyors were removed from their buying in the market, and provisions were bought by the clerk of the abbot, and all deficiencies were supplied out of the abbot's purse. The guests that ought to be entertained were received, and the honourable were honoured; the officials and monks, all of them alike, took their meals in the refectory, and on all sides superfluous charges were retrenched. However, some of the cloister monks said among themselves, "Seven, ay seven there were who devoured our substance, of whose devourings if any one did speak, he was accounted guilty of treason." Another would say, stretching forth his hands to heaven, "Blessed be God, who hath imparted this resolution to the abbot to correct such excesses"; and very many of them said that it was well done. Others would say, "Not so," they considering that such reform was an abatement of respect; and they styled the prudence of the abbot the ferocity of a wolf. Verily, they were again beginning to call their old dreams to mind, that the future abbot was to rage as a wolf.

The knights marvelled and the townsfolk marvelled at the things that came to pass, and some one of the common folk said, "It is a strange thing that so many monks and learned men should permit their possessions and rents to be confused and mingled with the possessions of the abbot; especially as they have been always accustomed to be kept distinct and apart from each other. It is strange also that they take no heed of the peril that may befall them after the death of the abbot if our lord the King should find them in such a condition."

Another person said that the abbot was the only one amongst them who acted wisely in the governing of external affairs, and that he ought to govern the whole who has the knowledge requisite to govern the whole. And there was one who said, "If there had been but one wise monk in such a large convent, who knew how to govern the house, the abbot would not have done as he has." And so we became a laughing-stock and a scoff to our neighbours.

About this time it came to pass that the anniversary obit of abbot Robert was to be sung in chapter, and it was ordered that a *placebo* and *dirige* should be sung more solemnly than ordinarily, namely, with tolling of the great bells, as upon the anniversaries of abbots Ording and Hugh, on account of the noble act of the aforesaid abbot Robert, who made the division between our possessions and rents, and the rents of the abbot. This solemnity, indeed, was performed by the advice of certain persons, so that thus at least the heart of the lord abbot might thus be stirred up to do what was right. There was also one who thought that this was done as a reproach to the abbot, who, it was said, was desirous of confusing and mingling together our and his possessions and rents, insomuch as he had seized the cellarership into his own hands. The abbot, however, hearing the unwonted noise of the bells, and well knowing and observing that it was done against all usage, discreetly ignored the reason of its being done, and solemnly chanted the mass.

Indeed, on the next Michaelmas day, desiring to appease the murmurings of certain persons, he appointed him who had been formerly sub-cellarer to be cellarer, and he ordered some other man to be named sub-cellarer; the aforesaid clerk, nevertheless, remaining with them, and managing all things as before. But when that clerk began to exceed the bounds of temperance, saying, "I am Bu," meaning the cellarer, when he had exceeded the bounds of temperance in drinking, and without the knowledge of the abbot was holding the court of the cellarer, taking gages and pledges, and receiving the annual rents, disbursing them by his own hand, he was called by the people the chief cellarer.

It was his habit to stroll about the court followed by a crowd of debtors, rich and poor, and of suitors of all ranks preferring various complaints, as if he were the master and high steward. On one such occasion, one of our officers happened to be standing in the court, and, upon seeing this, for confusion and shame, he wept outright, considering that this was a disgrace to our church, pondering upon the peril consequent thereon, and realizing that a clerk was preferred to a monk, to the prejudice of the whole convent.

Therefore some one, who shall be nameless, undertook, through a third party, that these things should be intimated to the abbot in a proper and reasonable manner; and he was given to understand that this species of arrogance in the clerk, which was committed to the disgrace and dishonour of the society, was very likely to breed a great disturbance and dissension in the convent. The abbot certainly did, when he heard of this, forthwith summon the cellarer and the aforesaid clerk before him, and gave orders that thenceforth the cellarer should consider himself as cellarer in receiving moneys, in holding pleas, and in all other things, save that the aforesaid clerk should assist him, not as an equal, but as a witness and adviser.

Hamo Blund, one of the wealthier men of this town, on his death-bed could hardly be persuaded to make a will. At last he did, but disposed of only three marks, and this in the hearing of no one, except his brother, wife and chaplain. The abbot, ascertaining this after the man's decease, called those three persons before him, and sharply rebuked them, especially upon this point, that the brother (who was his heir) and his wife would not suffer any one else to approach the sick man, they desiring to take all. The abbot said in audience, "I was his bishop, and had the charge of his soul; let not the folly of his priest and confessor turn to my peril. Insomuch as I could not advise the sick man when alive, I being absent, what concerns my conscience I shall now perform, late though it be. I therefore command that all his debts and his moveable chattels, which are worth, as it is said, two hundred marks, be reduced into a writing, and that one portion be given to the heir, and another to the wife, and the third to his poor kinsfolk and other poor persons. As to the horse which was led before the coffin of the deceased, and was offered to St. Edmund, I order that it be sent back and returned; for it does not beseem our church to be defiled with the gift of him who died intestate, and whom common report accuses of being habitually wont to put out his money to interest. By the face of God, if such a thing came to pass of any one again in my days, he shall not be buried in the churchyard!" On his saying these things, the others departed greatly disconcerted.

On the morrow of the Nativity of our Lord, there took place in the churchyard meetings, wrestlings, and matches, between the servants of the abbot and the burgesses of the town; and from words they came to blows, from cuffs to wounds and to the shedding of blood. The abbot, hearing of this, called to him privately certain of those who were present at the sight, but yet stood afar off, and ordered that the names of the evil-doers should be set down in writing. All these he caused to be summoned, that they should stand before him on the morrow of St. Thomas the archbishop, in the chapel of St. Denis, to answer therefor. Nor did he, in the meantime, invite to his own table any one of the burgesses, as he had been wont to do, on the first five days of Christmas.

On the day appointed, having taken the oaths from sixteen lawful men, and having heard their evidence, the abbot said, "It is manifest that these evil-doers have incurred the penalties of the canon *latæ sententiæ*, but because both parties are laymen, and do not understand what a crime it is to commit such a sacrilege as this, I shall by name and publicly excommunicate them, in order that others may be deterred from doing the like: and that in no wise there be any diminution of justice, I shall first begin with my own domestics and servants." And it was done accordingly, we putting on our robes and lighting the candles. So they all went forth from the church, and being advised so to do, they all stripped themselves, and altogether naked, except their drawers, they prostrated themselves before the door of the church.

When the assessors of the abbot had come, monks as well as clerks, and informed him, with tears in their eyes, that more than a hundred men were lying down thus naked, the abbot wept. Nevertheless, making a show of legal severity both in word and countenance and concealing the pity he felt, he desired to be persuaded by his counsellors that the penitents should be absolved, knowing that mercy is exalted over judgment, and that the church receives all penitents. Thereupon, they being all sharply whipped and absolved, they swore all of them that they would abide by the judgment of the church for sacrilege committed.

On the morrow, penance was assigned to them, according to the appointment of the canons; and thus the abbot restored all of them to unity of concord, uttering terrible threats to all those who by word or deed should furnish matter of discord.

Further, he publicly forbade meetings and shows to be had in the churchyard; and so all things being brought to a state of peace, the burgesses feasted on the following days with their lord the abbot, with great joy.

CHAPTER XII
THE CARES OF OFFICE

A COMMISSION of our lord the Pope had been directed to Hubert, Archbishop of Canterbury, and to the lord Bishop of Lincoln, and to Samson, Abbot of St. Edmund, touching the reformation of the church of Coventry, and the restoration of the monks thereto, without any revision of their case. The parties being summoned to Oxford, the judges received letters of request from our lord the King, that this business should be respited.

The archbishop and the bishop, seeming to know nothing, were silent, as if seeking the favour of the clerks. The abbot was the only one who spoke out, and he did so as a monk for the monks of Coventry, publicly advocating and defending their cause. And by his means it was so far proceeded with on that day, that a certain simple seisin was made to one of the monks of Coventry by delivery of one book. But corporate institution was deferred for a time, that so in some degree the abbot might obey the request of our lord the King.

At that time he entertained in his inn fourteen monks of Coventry who had appeared there; and when the monks were sitting at the table on one side of the house, and the masters of the schools who had been summoned thither on the other, the abbot was applauded as noble and liberal in his expenses. Never in all his life did he seem so joyful as at that time, for the reverence he bore towards reform of monastic rule. The feast of St. Hilary being now at hand, the abbot journeyed on to Coventry in high spirits, neither was he overcome by fatigue or charges, for he said, that even if he had to be carried in a horse-litter, he would not remain behind. On his arrival at Coventry, where for five days he was waiting for the archbishop, he kept with him all the afore-named monks, with their servants, in most honourable fashion, until a new prior was created, and the monks had been formally inducted. "He that hath ears to hear, let him hear," for it is an act worthy to be had in remembrance.

After this the abbot Samson and Robert of Scales came to an agreement concerning the moiety of the advowson of the church of Wetherden, and the same Robert acknowledged it to be the right of St. Edmund and the abbot. Thereupon the abbot, without any previous understanding taking place, and without any promise previously made, gave that moiety which belonged to him to Master Roger of Scales, brother of the same knight, upon this condition, that he should pay by the hand of our sacrist an annual pension of three marks to that master of the schools who should teach in the town of St. Edmund. This the abbot did, being induced thereto by motives of remarkable generosity; in order that as he had formerly purchased stone houses for the use of the schools, that poor clerks should be free from house rent, so now from thenceforth they might be freed from all demand of moneys which the master of the school demanded by custom for his teaching. And so, by God's will, and during the abbot's life, the entire moiety of the aforesaid church, which is worth, as it is said, one hundred shillings, was appropriated to such purposes.

Now the abbot, after that he had built in his vills throughout the abbacy many and various edifices, and had taken up his quarters at his manor houses oftener and more frequently than with us at home, at length, as if returning to himself, and as if making good better, said that he would stay more at home than he had been used to do; and would now erect some buildings within the court for necessary purposes, having regard to internals and externals, and as if he was aware that "the presence of the master is the profit of the field." Therefore he gave directions that the stables and offices in the court lodge and round about the same, formerly covered with reeds, should be newly roofed, and covered with tiles, under the supervision of Hugh the sacrist, so that thus all fear and risk of fire might be prevented.

And now, behold the acceptable time, the day of desire, whereof I write not but with great joy, myself having the care of the guests. Lo! at the command of the abbot the court lodge resounds with spades and masons' tools, for pulling down the guest-house; and now it is almost all levelled. Of the rebuilding, let the Most High take thought! The abbot built for himself a new larder in the court lodge, and gave to the convent the old larder (which was situated, in a very slovenly fashion, under the dorter) for the accommodation of the chamberlain. The chapels of St. Andrew and St. Katherine and St. Faith were newly covered with lead; many repairs were also made, both inside the church and without. If you do not believe, open your eyes and see. Also in his time our almonry, which previously was of wood and out of repair, was built in stone; whereto a certain brother of ours, Walter the physician, at that time almoner, contributed much of what he had acquired by his practice of physic.

The abbot also observing that the silver retable of the high altar, and many other precious ornaments, had been alienated for the purpose of the recovery of Mildenhall and the ransom of King Richard, was not desirous of replacing that table or such-like matters, which upon a similar occasion were liable to be torn away and misappropriated. He therefore turned his attention to the making of a most valuable cresting for the shrine of the glorious martyr Edmund, that his ornament might be set in a place whence it could by no possibility be abstracted, and whereon no human being would dare to put forth his hand.

For indeed, when King Richard was captive in Germany, there was no treasure in England that had not either to be given up or redeemed; yet the shrine of St. Edmund remained untouched. However, the question was raised before the justices of the exchequer, whether the shrine of St. Edmund should not, at least in part, be stripped for the ransom of King Richard. But the abbot standing up, answered, "Know ye of a surety, that this never shall be done by me, nor is there a man who can compel me to consent to it. But I will open the doors of the church: let him enter who will, let him approach who dare." Each of the justices replied with oaths, "I will not venture to approach it." "Nor will I." "St. Edmund grievously punishes those who are far off as well as those who are near at hand; how much more will he inflict vengeance upon those who take away his vesture!"

Upon this neither was the shrine despoiled, nor redemption paid. Therefore passing by other things, the abbot carefully and advisedly turned his mind towards the making of a cresting for the shrine. And now the plates of gold and silver resound between the hammer and the anvil, and "the carpenters wield their tools."

Adam of Cockfield dying, left for his heir a daughter of three months old; and the abbot gave the wardship of his fee to whom he would. Now King Richard, being solicited by some of his courtiers, anxiously sought for the wardship and the child for the benefit of one of his servants; at one time by letters, at another time by messengers.

But the abbot answered that he had given the ward away, and had confirmed his gift by his charter. Sending his own messenger to the King, he did all he could, by entreaty and good offices, to mitigate his wrath. And the King made answer, with great indignation, that he would avenge himself upon that proud abbot who had thwarted him, were it not for reverence of St. Edmund, whom he feared. When the messenger returned, the abbot very wisely passed over the King's threats without notice, and said, "Let the King send, if he will, and seize the ward; he has the strength and power of doing his will, indeed of taking away the whole of the abbacy. I shall never be bent to his will in this matter, nor by me shall this ever be done. For the thing that is most to be apprehended is, lest such things be made a precedent to the prejudice of my successors. On this business I will never give the King money. Let the Most High look to it. Whatever may befall, I will patiently bear."

Whilst, therefore, many were saying and believing that the King was exasperated against the abbot, lo! the King wrote in a friendly way to the abbot, and requested that he would give him some of his dogs. The abbot, not unmindful of that saying of the wise man—

Gifts, believe me, influence both men and gods, By the offer of gifts
Jove himself is appeased—

sent the dogs as the King requested, and moreover, added some horses
and other valuable gifts. The King graciously accepted them, and in public
most highly commended the honesty and fidelity of the abbot.

He also sent to the abbot by his messengers, as a token of intimacy and
affection, a ring of great price, which our lord the Pope, Innocent the Third,
of his great grace had given him, being indeed the very first gift that had been
offered after his consecration. Also, by his writ, the King rendered him many
thanks for the presents the abbot had sent him.

CHAPTER XIII
THE CUSTOMS OF THE TOWNSHIP

MANY persons marvelled at the changes in the customs that took place by the order or permission of the lord abbot Samson. From the time when the town of St. Edmund received the name and liberty of a borough, the men of every house used to give to the cellarer one penny in the beginning of August, to reap our corn, which annual payment was called rep-silver. Before the town became free, all of them used to reap as serfs; the dwellings of knights and chaplains, and of the servants of the court lodge being alone exempt from this payment. In process of time, the cellarer spared certain of the most wealthy of the town, demanding nothing from them. The other burgesses, seeing this, used openly to say that no one who had a dwelling house of his own was liable to pay this penny, but only those who rented houses from others.

Afterwards, they all in common sought this exemption, conferring thereon with the lord abbot, and offering an annual rent as a composition of this demand. The abbot, indeed, considering the undignified way in which the cellarer used to go through the town to collect rep-silver, and the manner in which he used to take distresses in the houses of the poor, sometimes taking trivets, sometimes doors, and sometimes other utensils, and how the old women came out with their distaffs, threatening and abusing the cellarer and his men, ordered that twenty shillings should be given every year to the cellarer at the next portman-moot, at the hand of the bailiff before August, by the burgesses, who were to pay the rent to discharge this. And it was done accordingly, and confirmed by our charter, there being given to them another quittance from a certain customary payment, which is called sorpeni, in consideration of four shillings, payable at the same term. For the cellarer was accustomed to receive one penny by the year for every cow belonging to the men of the town for their dung and pasture (unless perchance they happened to be the cows of the chaplains or of the servants at the court lodge). These cows he used to impound, and had great trouble in the matter.

Afterwards, indeed, when the abbot made mention of this in the chapter, the convent was very angry, and took it in ill part, so much so that Benedict the sub-prior in the chapter, answering for all, said, "That man, abbot Ording, who lies there, would not have done such a thing for five hundred marks of silver." The abbot, although he himself felt angry, put off the matter for a time.

There arose also a great contention between Roger the cellarer and Hugh the sacrist concerning the appurtenances of their offices, so that the sacrist would not lend to the cellarer the prison of the town for the purpose of detaining therein the thieves who were taken in the cellarer's jurisdiction. The cellarer was thereby oftentimes harassed, and because the thieves escaped he was reprimanded for default of justice.

Now it came to pass that one holding as a free tenant of the cellarer, dwelling without the gate, by name Ketel, was charged with theft, and being vanquished in a trial by battle, was hanged. The convent was grieved by the offensive words of the burgesses, who said that if that man had only dwelt within the borough, it would not have come to the ordeal, but that he would have acquitted himself by the oaths of his neighbours, as is the privilege of those who dwell within the borough. Therefore the abbot and the more reasonable part of the convent seeing this, and bearing in mind that the men without the borough as well as those within are ours, and ought all of them in like manner to enjoy the same liberty within the jurisdiction, except the villeins of Hardwick and their like, deliberately took thought with themselves how this could be done.

Thereupon the abbot, being desirous of limiting the offices of the sacristy and the cellary by certain articles, and of quieting all contentions, commanded, as if taking the part of the sacrist, that the servants of the town bailiff and the servants of the cellarer should together enter upon the fee of the cellarer for the purpose of seizing thieves and malefactors, and that the bailiff should have half the profit for their imprisonment and safe keeping and for his pains therein; and that the court of the cellarer should go to the portman-moot, and judge the prisoners in common. It was also ordered that the men of the cellarer should come to the toll-house with the others, and there renew their pledges, and should be inscribed upon the bailiff's roll, and should there give the bailiff that penny which is called borth-selver, whereof the cellarer was to have one half part; but at this time the cellarer receives nothing at all from this. The intent of all this was, that every one should enjoy equal privilege. Nevertheless, the burgesses at this time say, that the dwellers in the outskirts ought not to be quit of toll in market, unless they belong to the merchant's guild. Moreover, the bailiff (the abbot conniving at the matter) now claims for himself the fines and forfeitures accruing from the fee of the cellarer.

The ancient customs of the cellarer, which we have seen, were these: The cellarer had his messuage and barns near Scurun's well, at which place he was accustomed to exercise his jurisdiction upon robbers, and hold his court for all pleas and plaints. Also at that place he was accustomed to put his men in pledge, and to enroll them and to renew their pledges every year, and to take such profit therefor as the bailiff of the town was to take at the portman-moot. This messuage, with the adjacent garden, now in the occupation of the infirmarer, was the mansion of Beodric, who was of old time the lord of this town, and after whom also the town came to be called Beodricsworth. His demesne lands are now in the demesne of the cellarer, and that which is now called averland was the land of his rustics. And the total amount of the holding of himself and his churls was thirty times thirty acres of land, which are still the fields of this town.

The service thereof, when the town was made free, was divided into two parts, so that the sacrist or town bailiff was to receive a free annual payment, namely, for each acre twopence. The cellarer was to have the ploughings and other services, namely, the ploughing of one rood for each acre, without meals (which custom is still observed), and was to have the folds wherein all the men of the town, except the steward, who has his own fold, are bound to put their sheep (which custom also is still observed); and was to have aver-peni, namely, for each thirty acres twopence (which custom was done away with before the decease of abbot Hugh, when Gilbert of Elveden was cellarer).

Furthermore, the men of the town were wont upon the order of the cellarer to go to Lakenheath, and bring back a day's catch of eels from Southrey. They often, indeed, used to return empty-handed, so they had their trouble without any profit to the cellarer. It was therefore settled between them that each thirty acres, from thenceforth, should pay one penny by the year, and the men were to remain at home. But, in fact, at this time, those lands are subdivided into so many parts, that it can hardly be ascertained by whom that annual payment is to be made; so that I have seen the cellarer, in one year, receive twenty-seven pence, but now he can hardly get tenpence halfpenny.

The cellarer was also wont to exercise authority over the ways without the town, so that it was not lawful for any one to dig for chalk or clay without his licence. He also was accustomed to summon the fullers of the town, that they should furnish cloth for his salt. Otherwise he would prohibit them the use of the waters, and would seize the webs he found there; which customs are still observed. Also, whosoever bought corn, or indeed anything from the cellarer, was accustomed to be quit from toll at the gate of the town when he went homewards, wherefore the cellarer sold his produce dearer; which usage is still observed. Also, the cellarer is accustomed to take toll of flax at the time of its carrying, namely, one truss from each load. Also, the cellarer alone ought, or at least used to have, a free bull in the fields of the town; now many persons have bulls.

Also, when any one surrendered his burgage land in alms to the convent, and this was assigned to the cellarer, or other official, that land used, thenceforth, to be quit of haggovele, and most especially so to the cellarer, on account of the dignity of his office, for he is the second father in the monastery, or even as a matter of reverence to the convent, for the estate of those who procure our provisions ought to be favourable. But the abbot says that usage is unjust, because the sacrist loses his service. Further, the cellarer was accustomed to warrant to the servants of the court lodge, that they should be quit of scot and tallage; but now it is not so, for the burgesses say that the servants of the court lodge ought to be quit only so far as they are servants, but not when they hold burgage in the town, and when they or their wives publicly buy and sell in the market.

Also, the cellarer was used freely to take all the dunghills in the street, for his own use, unless it were before the doors of those who were holding averland; for to them only was it allowable to collect dung, and to keep it. This custom gradually lapsed in the time of abbot Hugh until Dennis and Roger of Hingham became cellarers. Being desirous of reviving the ancient custom, they took the cars of the burgesses laden with dung, and made them unload; but a multitude of the burgesses resisting, and being too strong for them, every one in his own tenement now collects his dung in a heap, and the poor sell theirs when and to whom they choose.

The cellarer was also wont to have this privilege in the market of this town, that he and his purveyors should have pre-emption of all the provisions for the use of the convent, if the abbot were not at home. Also, that the purveyors of the abbot, or cellarer, whichever of them first came into the market, should buy first, either the latter without the former, or the former without the latter. But if both were present, then preference was to be given to the abbot. Also, in the season when herrings were sold, the purveyors of the abbot should always buy a hundred herrings at a halfpenny less than other people, and likewise the cellarer and his purveyors. Also, if a load of fish or other provisions should come first into the court lodge, or into the market, and that load should not have been discharged from the horse or from the cart, the cellarer or his purveyors might buy the whole and take it home with them without paying toll. But the abbot Samson commanded his purveyors that they should give preference to the cellarer and his men, because, as he himself said, he had much rather himself go without than his convent. Therefore the purveyors, "in honour preferring one another," if they find there is any one thing to be bought which is not enough for both parties, buy it between them, and divide it, share and share alike, and so between the head and the members, and the father and the sons, there remains an agreement in disagreement.

The poet has said, "Envy aims at the highest," and it is for this reason that I repeat these words, that when some one was perusing this narrative, and while he was reading of so many good acts, he called me a flatterer of the abbot, and a seeker of favour and grace, saying that I had silently suppressed some things which ought not to have been passed by.

When I inquired which and what sort of acts they might be, he answered, "Do you not see how the abbot grants away, at his own good pleasure, the escheats of land belonging to the demesnes of the convent, and the female heirs of lands, and the widows, as well within the town of St. Edmund as without? Also, do you not see how the abbot draws to himself the plaints and pleas of those who demand by the King's writ lands which are of the fee of the convent, and especially those plaints from which profit arises; and those from which no gain ensues, he turns over to the cellarer or sacrist, or other officials?" Whereto I answered, as I believe the fact to be, perhaps rightly, perhaps wrongly, and said that every lord of a fee whereto there is homage, ought by right to have an escheat whenever it shall have fallen within the fee in respect whereof he has received homage. By parity of reason, there is due to him general aid of the burgesses, and also the wardships of boys, and the gifts of widows and girls, in those fees in respect whereof he has received homage; for all these things seem to belong to the abbot alone, unless by chance the abbey shall be vacant.

Moreover, in the town of St. Edmund a special custom has place, by reason of its being a borough, that the next in blood shall have the wardship of a boy with an inheritance, until the years of discretion. Furthermore, I thus answered him concerning the plaints and pleas, that I had never seen the abbot usurp jurisdiction that belonged to us, unless in default of our administering justice; but nevertheless, he had on some occasions taken money, in order that by the intervention of his authority plaints and pleas should attain their final determination. Also, I have sometimes seen pleas which belonged to us decided in the court of the abbot, because there was not any in the commencement of the suit who would, on the part of the convent, assert jurisdiction.

CHAPTER XIV
THE SHRINE OF ST. EDMUND

IN the year of grace one thousand one hundred and ninety-eight, the glorious martyr Edmund was pleased to strike terror into our convent, and to instruct us that his body should be kept more reverently and diligently than it had hitherto been.

There was a wooden platform between the shrine and the high altar, whereon stood two tapers, which the keepers of the shrine used to renew and stick together, by placing one candle upon the stump of another in a slovenly manner. Under this platform there were many things irreverently huddled together, such as flax and thread and wax, and various utensils. In fact, whatever was used by the keepers of the shrine was put there, for there was a door with iron gratings.

Now, when these keepers of the shrine were fast asleep, on the night of St. Etheldreda, part of a candle that had been renewed, and was still burning, fell, as we conjecture, upon the aforesaid platform covered with rags. Consequently, all that was near, above or below, began to burn rapidly, so much so that the iron gratings were at a white heat. And lo! the wrath of the Lord was kindled, but not without mercy, according to that saying, "In wrath remember mercy"; for just then the clock struck before the hour of matins, and the master of the vestry getting up, observed and noticed the fire. He ran at once, and, striking the gong as if for a dead person, cried at the top of his voice that the shrine was consumed by fire.

We then, all running thither, found the fire raging wonderfully, and encircling the whole shrine, and almost reaching the woodwork of the church. Our young men, running for water, some to the well, some to the clock, some with their hoods, not without great labour, extinguished the force of the fire, and also stripped some of the altars upon the first alarm. And when cold water was poured upon the front of the shrine, the stones fell, and were reduced almost to powder. Moreover, the nails by which the plates of silver were affixed to the shrine started from the wood, which had been burnt underneath to the thickness of my finger, and the plates of silver were left dangling one from the other without nails. However, the golden image of the Majesty in front of the shrine, together with some of the stonework, remained firm and untouched, and brighter after the fire than it was before, for it was all of gold.

It so happened, by the will of the Highest, that at that time the great beam which used to be over the altar had been removed, in order to be adorned with new carving. It also happened that the cross, the small image of St. Mary and St. John, the chest with the shirt of St. Edmund, and the reliquaries and other shrines which used to hang from the same beam, and other holy things which also stood upon the beam, had every one of them been previously taken away. Otherwise all these would have been burnt, as we believe, even as a painted cloth was burnt which hung in the place of this beam. But what would it have been had the church been curtained?

When, therefore, we had assured ourselves that the fire had in no place penetrated the shrine, by carefully inspecting the chinks and crannies, if there were any, and had perceived that all was cold, our grief in a great measure abated: but all at once some of our brethren cried out with a great wailing, that the cup of St. Edmund had been burnt. When many of us were searching here and there for the stones and plates among the coals and cinders, they drew forth the cup entirely uninjured, lying in the middle of the great charred timbers, which were then put out, and found the same wrapped up in a linen cloth, half burnt. But the oaken box in which the cup was usually placed had been burnt to ashes, and only the iron bands and iron lock were found. When we saw this miracle, we all wept for joy.

Now, as we observed that the greater part of the front of the shrine was stripped off, and abhorring the disgraceful circumstances of the fire, after a general consultation we sent for a goldsmith, and caused the metal plates to be joined together and fixed to the shrine without the least delay, to avoid the scandal of the matter. We also caused all traces of the fire to be covered over with wax or in some other way. But the Evangelist testifies that "there is nothing covered which shall not be revealed": for some pilgrims came very early in the morning to make their offerings, who could have perceived nothing of the sort. Nevertheless, certain of them, peering about, inquired where was the fire that they had just heard had been about the shrine. And since it could not be entirely concealed, it was answered to these inquirers that a candle had fallen down and that three napkins had been burnt, and that by the heat of the fire some of the stonework in front of the shrine had been destroyed. Yet for all this there went forth a lying rumour, that the head of the saint had been burnt. Some indeed contented themselves with saying that the hair only was singed; but afterwards, the truth being known, "the mouth of them that spake lies was stopped."

All these things came to pass by God's providence, in order that the places round about the shrine of His saint should be more decently kept, and that the purpose of the lord abbot should be sooner and without delay carried into execution; which was, that the shrine itself, together with the body of the holy martyr, should be placed with greater security, and with more pomp, in a more dignified position. For before this aforesaid mishap occurred, the cresting of the shrine was half finished, and the marble blocks whereon the shrine was to be elevated and was to rest, were for the most part ready and polished.

The abbot, who at this time was absent, was exceedingly grieved at these reports; and he on his return home, going into the chapter-house, declared that these and the like, nay, much greater perils might befall us for our sins, more especially for our grumbling about our meat and drink; in a certain measure turning the blame upon the whole body of the convent, rather than upon the avarice and carelessness of the keepers of the shrine. To the intent that he might induce us to abstain from our pittances for at least one year, and to apply, for at least a year, the rents of the pittancy, for the purpose of repairing the front of the shrine with pure gold, he himself first showed us an example of liberality by giving all the treasure of gold he possessed, namely, fifteen golden rings, worth, as it was believed, sixty marks, in our presence, towards the reparation of the shrine.

We, on the other hand, all agreed to give our pittancy for such purpose; but our resolution was afterwards altered, by the sacrist saying that St. Edmund could very well repair his shrine without such assistance.

At this time there came a man of great account, but who he was I know not, that related to the abbot a vision he had seen, whereat he himself was much moved. Indeed, he related the same in full chapter, with a very bitter speech. "It is indeed true," he said, "that a certain great man has seen a vision, to wit, that he saw the holy martyr St. Edmund lie outside his shrine, and with groans say that he was despoiled of his clothes, and was wasted away by hunger and thirst; and that his churchyard and the courts of his church were negligently kept."

This dream the abbot expounded to us all publicly, laying the blame upon us, in this fashion: "St. Edmund alleges that he is naked, because you defraud the naked poor of your old clothes, and because you give with reluctance what you are bound to give them, and it is the same with your meat and drink. Moreover, the idleness and negligence of the sacrist and his associates, are apparent from the recent misfortune by fire which has taken place between the shrine and the altar." On hearing this the convent was very sorrowful; and after chapter several of the brethren met together, and interpreted the dream after this fashion: "We," said they, "are the naked members of St. Edmund, and the convent is his naked body; for we are despoiled of our ancient customs and privileges. The abbot has everything, the chamberlainship, the sacristy, the cellary; while we perish of hunger and thirst, because we have not our victuals, save by the clerk of the abbot and by his ministration. If the keepers of the shrine have been negligent, let the abbot lay it to his own charge, for it was he who appointed such careless fellows."

In such wise spoke many in the convent. But when this interpretation of the dream was communicated to the abbot, in the forest of Harlow, on his way from London, he was very wroth, and was troubled in mind, and made answer: "They will wrest that dream against me, will they? By the face of God! so soon as I reach home I will restore to them the customs that they say are theirs. I will withdraw my clerk from the cellary, and will leave them to themselves; and I shall see the fruits of their wisdom at the end of the year. This year I have been residing at home, and I have caused their cellary to be managed without incurring debt; and this is the way in which they render me thanks."

On the abbot's return home, having it in purpose to translate the blessed martyr, he humbled himself before God and man, meditating within himself how he might reform himself, and make himself at peace with all men, especially with his own convent. Therefore, sitting in chapter, he commanded that a cellarer and sub-cellarer should be chosen by our common assent, and withdrew his own clerk, saying, that whatsoever he had done he had done it for our advantage, as he called God and his saints to witness, and justified himself in various ways.

"Hear, O Heaven!" the things that I speak; "give ear, O earth!" to what Abbot Samson did. The feast of St. Edmund now approaching, the marble blocks were polished, and everything made ready for the elevation of the shrine. The feast day having therefore been kept on a Friday, a three days' fast was proclaimed on the following Sunday to the people, and the occasion of the fast was publicly explained. The abbot also announced to the convent that they should prepare themselves for transferring the shrine, and placing it upon the high altar, until the masons' work was finished; and he appointed the time and the manner for doing this work.

When we had that night come to matins, there stood the great shrine upon the altar, empty within, adorned with white doeskins above, below, and round about, which were fixed to the wood by silver nails; but one panel stood below, by a column of the church, and the sacred body still lay in its accustomed place. Lauds having been sung, we all proceeded to take our disciplines. This being performed, the lord abbot and those with him vested themselves in albs; and approaching reverently, as it was fit they should, they hastened to uncover the coffin.

First there was an outer cloth of linen, overwrapping the coffin and all. This was found tied on the upper side with strings of its own. Within this was a cloth of silk, and then another linen cloth, and then a third. And so at last the coffin was uncovered, standing upon a tray of wood, that the bottom of it might not be injured by the stone.

Affixed to the outside, over the breast of the martyr, lay an angel of gold, about the length of a man's foot, holding in one hand a golden sword and in the other a banner. Underneath it, there was a hole in the lid of the coffin, where the ancient custodians of the martyr had been wont to lay their hands, for the purpose of touching the sacred body. And over the figure of the angel was this verse inscribed:—

"Martiris ecce zoma servat Michaelis agalma."

(*"Behold the martyr's body St. Michael's image keeps."*)

At the two heads of the coffin were iron rings, as there used to be on Danish chests.

So, raising up the coffin with the body, they carried it to the altar, and I lent thereto my sinful hand to help in carrying it, although the abbot had strictly commanded that no one should approach unless he was called. The coffin was placed within the shrine, and the panel was put thereon and fastened down.

Now we all began to think that the abbot would exhibit the coffin to the people on the octave of the feast, and would replace the sacred body before all of us. But we were sadly deceived, as the sequel will show; for on Wednesday, while the convent was singing compline, the abbot spoke with the sacrist and Walter the physician, and it was resolved that twelve brethren should be appointed who were strong enough to carry the panels of the shrine, and skilful in fixing and unfixing them.

The abbot then said that it had been the object of his prayers to see his patron saint, and that he wished to join with him the sacrist and Walter the physician when he looked upon him; and there were also nominated the abbot's two chaplains, the two keepers of the shrine, and the two keepers of the vestry, with six others, Hugh the sacrist, Walter the physician, Augustine, William of Diss, Robert and Richard. The convent being all asleep, these twelve vested themselves in albs, and drawing the coffin out of the shrine, carried and placed it upon a table near where the shrine used to be, and commenced unfastening the lid, which was joined and fixed to the coffin with sixteen very long iron nails. When, with considerable difficulty, they had performed this, all were ordered to go further away, except the two forenamed associates.

Now the coffin was so filled with the sacred body, both in length and width, that even a needle could hardly be put between the head and the wood or between the feet and the wood. The head lay united to the body, somewhat raised by a small pillow. The abbot, looking attentively, next found a silk cloth veiling the whole body, and then a linen cloth of wondrous whiteness, and upon the head a small linen cloth, and after that another small and very fine silken cloth, as if it had been the veil of some nun. Lastly, they discovered the body, wound round with a linen cloth, and then it was that all the lineaments of the saint's body were laid open to view.

At this point the abbot stopped, saying he durst not proceed further, or view the holy body naked. Taking the head between his hands, he sighed and spoke thus: "Glorious martyr, St. Edmund, blessed be the hour wherein thou wast born! Glorious martyr, turn not my boldness to my perdition, for that I, miserable sinner, do touch thee, for thou knowest my devotion and my intention!" And proceeding, he touched the eyes and the nose, which was very massive and prominent. Then he touched the breast and arms, and raising the left arm, he touched the fingers, and placed his own fingers between the fingers of the saint. Proceeding further, he found the feet standing stiff up, like the feet of a man who had died that day, and he touched the toes, and in touching counted them.

It was then proposed that the other brethren should be called forward, in order that they might see these wonders; and six, being thus called, approached, and also six other brethren with them, who had stolen in without the abbot's assent, and saw the saint's body, namely, Walter of St. Alban's, Hugh the infirmarer, Gilbert the brother of the prior, Richard of Hingham, Jocell the cellarer, and Thurstan the little, who alone put forth his hand, and touched the feet and knees of the saint. And the Most High so ordering it, that there might be abundance of witnesses, one of our brethren, John of Diss, sitting upon the roof of the church with the servants of the vestry, saw all these things plainly enough.

All this being done, the lid was fastened down on the coffin with the same, and with the same number of nails, and in like manner as before, the martyr being covered up with the same cloths and in the same order as he was when first discovered. Finally, the coffin was placed in the accustomed place, and there was put upon the coffin, near to the angel, a certain silken bag, wherein was deposited a schedule written in English, containing certain salutations of Ailwin the monk, as is believed, which schedule was found close by the golden angel when the coffin was uncovered. By the abbot's order, there was forthwith written another short memorandum, also deposited in the same bag, in the following form of words: "In the year of the incarnation of our Lord, 1198, the abbot Samson, upon the impulse of devotion, saw and touched the body of St. Edmund on the night after the feast of St. Catherine, these being witnesses." And thereto were subscribed the names of the eighteen monks.

The brethren also wound the whole coffin up in a suitable linen cloth, and over the same placed a new and most valuable silken cloth, which Hubert, Archbishop of Canterbury, had offered at the shrine that very year, and they placed lengthwise a certain linen cloth doubled under it and next to the stone, to prevent the coffin or the tray whereon it stood from being injured by the stone. Afterwards the panels were brought forth, and properly joined together on the shrine.

When the convent assembled to sing matins, and understood what had been done, all who had not seen these things were very sorrowful, saying among themselves, "We have been sadly deceived." However, after matins had been sung, the abbot called the convent to the high altar, and briefly recounting what had been done, alleged that he ought not to call—and could not call—all of them to be present on such an occasion. Hearing this, with tears we sang "Te Deum laudamus," and hastened to ring the bells in the choir.

On the fourth day after, the abbot deposed the keepers of the shrine and the keeper of St. Botolph, appointing new ones, and establishing rules, so that the holy places should be more carefully and diligently kept. He also caused the great altar, which heretofore was hollow, and wherein many things were irreverently stowed away, and that space which was between the shrine and the altar, to be made solid with stone and cement, so that no danger from fire could arise by the negligence of the keepers, as had been already the case; according to the saying of the wise man, who said,

"Happy is he who learns caution from the danger of others."

CHAPTER XV
THE MONASTERY IN REVOLT

NOW when the abbot had obtained the favour and grace of King Richard by gifts and money, so that he had good reason to believe that he could succeed according to his desire in all his undertakings, the King died, and the abbot lost his labour and outlay. However, King John, immediately after his coronation, setting aside all other affairs, came down to St. Edmund, drawn thither by his vow and by devotion. We, indeed, believed that he was come to make offering of some great matter; but all he offered was one silken cloth, which his servants had borrowed from our sacrist, and to this day have not paid for. He availed himself of the hospitality of St. Edmund, which was attended with enormous expense, and upon his departure bestowed nothing at all, either of honour or profit, upon the saint, save thirteen pence sterling, which he offered at his mass on the day of his departure.

About that time some of our officials made complaint, stating in our chapter that Ralph the porter, our servant, maintained causes and actions against them to the damage of the church and to the prejudice of the convent. It was ordered by the prior, with the assent of us all, that he should be punished according to the custom whereby our servants are usually punished, that is, by the withholding of their stipends. It was therefore ordered that the cellarer should withhold from him, not the corody which of right belonged to his office according to the tenour of his charter, but certain additions and perquisites which the cellarer and sub-cellarer allowed him without knowledge of the convent at large. Now the aforesaid Ralph, accompanied by certain of the abbot's table, complained to the abbot on his return from London, that the prior and convent had disseised him of his corody, whereof he was seised when the abbot had first come to the abbacy. They also stated to the abbot that this act was done without his sanction, and to his dishonour, and unreasonably, without his advice, and without investigation. The abbot indeed believed him, and, in other wise than was either fitting or customary, became excited. He instantly justified Ralph, and affirmed that he was innocent. Coming into chapter and complaining thereof, he said that what had been done was to his prejudice and without his consent. And it was answered by one of us, the others all joining him, that this was done by the prior, and with the assent of the whole convent.

The abbot was confused at this, saying, "I have nourished and brought up children, and they have rebelled against me." Not overlooking this (as he ought to have done) for the sake of peace to the many, but rather exhibiting his power with a resolution not to be over-mastered, he openly gave command to the cellarer that he should restore to Ralph, fully and wholly, all that had been taken from him, and that he should drink nothing but water till he had restored everything. But Jocell the cellarer, hearing this, chose for that day to drink water, rather than restore the corody to Ralph against the will of the convent. When this came to the abbot's knowledge on the morrow, he forbade both meat and drink to the cellarer until he restored all. With these words the abbot immediately departed from the town, and stayed away for eight days.

On the same day on which the abbot had departed, the cellarer arose in chapter, and exhibiting the precept of the abbot, and holding his keys in his hand, said that he had rather be deposed from his office than do anything in opposition to the convent. And then there began a great tumult in the convent, such as I had never before seen; and they said that the precept of the abbot was not to be obeyed. But the seniors and more prudent men of the convent, discreetly holding their tongues, upon being urged gave it as their opinion that the abbot was to be obeyed in everything, except in things manifestly against God's pleasure; and intimated that we must bear with this scandalous behaviour for a time for the sake of peace, lest worse should befall. Now when the prior had begun to sing "Verba mea" for all deceased, as is the rule, the novices withstood him, and with them nearly the half of the convent; and raising their voices, they all cried out in answer, and opposed it. Nevertheless, the senior part of the convent prevailed, although they were few as compared with the rest.

The abbot, although absent, yet by his messengers terrified some by threats. Some others he drew over to him by fair words; and the more influential men of the convent, as though they were afraid even of his garment, he caused to secede from the counsel of the generality, that that gospel should be fulfilled which says, "Every kingdom divided against itself is brought to desolation." Moreover, the abbot said that he would by no means come amongst us, by reason of the conspiracies and oaths which, as he said, we had made against him, that we should kill him with our knives. However, returning home, and sitting in his inner chamber, he gave orders to one of our brethren whom he vehemently suspected, that he should come to him; and because he would not come, fearing to be taken and bound, he was excommunicated; and the whole day after he was put into fetters, remaining till morning in the infirmary. Three others the abbot also included in a lighter sentence, in order that the others might fear.

On the morrow it was resolved that the abbot should be sent for, and that we should humble ourselves before him, both in word and demeanour, so that his anger might be appeased; and it was done accordingly. He, on the other hand, answering meekly enough, but always alleging his own rectitude, laid the blame upon us. Yet when he saw that we were willing to be overcome, was himself fairly overcome. Bursting into tears, he swore that he had never grieved for any one thing as he had upon the present occasion, as well on his own account as on our account also, and more especially for the scandal, the evil report which had already gone abroad concerning our dissension, to the effect that the monks of St. Edmund wished to kill their abbot.

And when the abbot had told us how he went away on purpose till his anger had cooled, repeating this saying of the philosopher, "I would have taken vengeance upon thee had I not been angry," he arose, weeping, and embraced all and every one of us with the kiss of peace. He wept, and we also wept. The brethren who had been excommunicated were immediately absolved; and thus "the tempest ceased, and there was a great calm." Yet for all this the abbot gave private orders that the accustomed corody should be given without stint to Ralph the porter, as heretofore; to which matter, however, we shut our eyes, being at last made to understand that there is no lord who will not bear rule, and that battle is perilous which is undertaken against the stronger, and is begun against the more powerful party.

In the year of grace one thousand two hundred a marshalling took place of the knights of St. Edmund and of their fees, whereof their ancestors had been infeoffed.

Alberic de Vere holds five knights' fees and a half: namely, in Loddon and in Brome, one knight's fee; in Mendham and Preston, one knight's fee; in Rede, one knight's fee; and in Cockfield, half a knight's fee; and in Livermere, two knights' fees.

William of Hastings holds five knights' fees: to wit, in Lidgate, and in Blunham and in Harling, three knights' fees; and in Tibenham and in Gissing, two.

The Earl Roger holds three knights' fees in Norton and Brisingham.

Robert Fitz Roger holds one knight's fee in Marlesford.

Alexander of Kirkby holds one knight's fee in Kirkby.

Roger of Eu holds two knights' fees, in Mickfield and in Topscroft.

Arnald of Charneles and his co-parceners, one knight's fee, in Oakley, and in Quiddenham, and in Thurston, and Stuston.

Osbert of Wachesham, one knight's fee in Marlingford and in Wortham.

William of Tostock, one knight's fee in Randestune.

Gilbert Fitz Ralph, three knights' fees: namely, in Thelnetham and in Hepworth, one knight's fee; in Reydon (in Blithing) and in Gissing, one knight's fee; and in Saxham, one knight's fee.

Ralph of Buckenham, half a knight's fee in Buckenham.

William of Bardwell, two knights' fees in Barningham, and in Bardwell, and in Hunston, and in Stanton.

Robert of Langtoft holds three knights' fees, in Stow, and in Ashfield, and in Troston, and in Little Waltham in Essex.

Adam of Cockfield, two knights' fees: namely, in Lavenham, and in Onehouse, one knight's fee; and in Lelesey.

Robert Fitz Walter, one knight's fee, in Great Fakenham and in Sapiston.

William Blund, one knight's fee in Thorp (in Blackbourn).

Gilbert of Peche, two knights' fees: namely, in Waude and in Gedding, one knight's fee; in Felsham, and in Euston, and in Groton, one knight's fee.

Gilbert of St. Clare, two knights' fees, in Bradfield and in Wattisfield.

Geoffrey of Whelnetham and Gilbert of Manston, one knight's fee, in Whelnetham and in Manston.

Hubert of Ansty, half a knight's fee in Briddinghoe.

Gervase of Rothing, one knight's fee, in Chipley and in Rothing.

Robert of Halsted, one knight's fee in Halsted, and half a knight's fee in Brockley.

Reginald of Brockley, one knight's fee in Brockley.

Simon of Patteshall, half a knight's fee in Whatfield.

Peter Fitz Alan, half a knight's fee in Brockley.

Ralph of Presseni, half a knight's fee in Stanningfield.

Richard of Ickworth, two knights' fees, in Ickworth and in Wangford.

Robert of Horning, half a knight's fee in Horning.

Walter of Saxham, one knight's fee, in Ashfield and in Saxham.

William of Wordwell, half a knight's fee in Whelnetham.

Norman of Risby, half a knight's fee in Risby.

Peter of Livermere and Alan of Flempton, one knight's fee in Livermere and Ampton.

Roger of Morieux, one knight's fee in Thorpe.

Hugh of Eleigh, in Eleigh, and in Preston, and in Bradfield, two knights' fees.

Stephen of Brockdish, one fourth part of a knight's fee in Brockdish.

Adam of Barningham, one fourth part of a knight's fee in Barningham.

William of Wordwell, in Little Livermere and in Wordwell, one fourth part of a knight's fee.

The total is fifty-two fees and one-half and one quarter.

Now Geoffrey Ruffus, one of our monks, although he deported himself in somewhat too secular a manner, yet was a useful person to us in the keeping of the four manors of Barton, Pakenham, Rougham, and Bradfield, where there had often been heretofore a deficiency in the farms. But the abbot, although hearing of the evil report of his continence, yet winked at it for a long time, most likely because Geoffrey seemed to be serviceable to the community. At length, when the truth was known, the abbot suddenly made a seizure of his chests, put them in the vestry, and caused all the stock of the different manors to be kept most closely, and remanded Geoffrey to the cloister. There was found much gold and silver, to the value of two hundred marks, the whole of which the abbot said was to be laid by for the purpose of making the front of the shrine of St. Edmund.

On the feast of St. Michael it was decreed in chapter that two brethren, not one alone, should succeed to the keepership of the manors, whereof one was Roger of Hingham, who promised before us all that he was willing and able to undertake the charge of the manors and cellary together. The abbot gave his assent thereto, but the convent was reluctant. And Jocell, who had well and carefully managed his office, and for two years had been in charge of the cellary without incurring debt, as other cellarers had used to do, was deposed from the cellary and was made sub-cellarer. But at the end of the year, Roger, on rendering account of his receipts and outgoings, affirmed that he had received sixty marks from the stock of the manors to supply the deficiency of the cellarer. Therefore, upon counsel being taken, it was resolved that Jocell should be restored to the cellary; and Mildenhall and Chebenhall and Southwold were granted to him. The other manors were committed to Roger and Albin, and were divided from the cellary, lest the manors should be ruined by the cellary, or the cellary be ruined by the manors.

Adam of Cockfield being dead, the abbot could have had three hundred marks for the wardship of the only daughter of the same Adam; but because the grandfather of the damsel had taken her away privily, and inasmuch as the abbot was not able to obtain seisin of the damsel, unless by the aid of the archbishop, the abbot granted that wardship to Hubert, Archbishop of Canterbury, for the consideration of one hundred pounds. The archbishop, for five hundred marks, granted to Thomas de Burgh, the brother of the

King's chamberlain, that same wardship; and the damsel was delivered to him, with her rights, by the hand of the abbot. Thomas, therefore, at once required the seisin of these manors, which we had in our hands after the death of Adam—Cockfield, Semer, and Groton—we believing that we had power to retain all of them in our demesne, or at least two of them, Semer and Groton; both because Robert of Cockfield, being on his deathbed, had publicly affirmed that he could claim nothing by right of inheritance in these two manors, and also because Adam, his son, had re-assigned to us those two manors in full court, and had made his charter thereof, wherein it was contained that he holds those two manors by the permission of the convent during his life only.

Thomas, therefore, suing a writ of recognition thereof, caused the knights to be summoned, that they should come to be sworn before the King at Tewkesbury. Our charter read in public had no force, for the whole court was against us. The oath being administered, the knights said that they knew nothing about our charters, or of any private agreements; but this they said they did believe, that Adam and his father and his grandfather, for a hundred years back, had holden the manors in fee-farm, one after the other, on the days of their respective deaths. Thus we were disseised by the judgment of the court, after much trouble and many charges expended, saving nevertheless our ancient fee-farm rents payable annually.

The lord abbot seemed to be "misled by a certain appearance of right," because, forsooth, the Scripture saith, "I will not give my glory to another." The abbot of Cluny coming to us, and received by us in such wise as he ought, our abbot would not give place, either in chapter or in the procession on Sunday, but he must needs sit and stand in the middle between the abbot of Cluny and the abbot of Chertsey. Wherefore divers thought different things, and many expressed their feelings in various ways.

CHAPTER XVI
THE ELECTION OF A NEW PRIOR

ROBERT the prior was at this time in a dying state; but while he was yet alive many opinions were uttered as to appointing a new prior. Some one, therefore, related to us, that the abbot sitting in the choir, and steadfastly beholding all the brethren from the first to the last, found no one upon whom his spirit might rest to make him prior, save Herbert his chaplain. By these and similar acts the will of the abbot was made apparent to most of us. One of us hearing this, answered that it was not to be believed; asserting "that the abbot, a diligent and prudent man, to such a man, a youth and almost beardless novice of twelve years, who had only become a cloister monk four years ago, not approved in the cure of souls, nor in doctrinal learning—to such a one," said he, "he will never give the priorate."

Now, when the prior died, the abbot was staying in London; and a certain person said, "A month has scarcely elapsed since the abbot made Herbert the chaplain, sub-sacrist, and when he committed that office to him, in the chapel of St. Nicasius, he promised that if he could, by any means, make him prior, he would use his utmost exertions on his behalf." Some one hearing of this, who was desirous of making himself agreeable to the abbot and the future prior, most urgently solicited many of us, seniors and juniors alike, that when the opportunity presented itself they would nominate Herbert, at least with some others, for prior. He affirmed that by this means they would gratify the abbot, for such indeed was his desire.

There certainly were many of us, as well of the seniors as the juniors, who asserted that the same Herbert was an amiable and affable man, and worthy of much honour. Also, there were some—few in number, indeed, but whose advice was more respected, and who belonged to the wiser part of the convent—who were desirous of promoting Master Hermer the sub-prior to be prior, as being an experienced, learned and eloquent man, skilful and expert in the cure of souls, who at that time had governed the cloister for fourteen years in good discipline, an approved sub-prior, and well known. This man, I say, they were desirous of preferring, according to that saying of the wise man, "believe an experienced master."

But the greater number of us secretly grumbled in opposition, saying that he was a passionate, impatient, restless, fussy and fretful man, a litigious person, and a disturber of peace, deriding him, and saying, "The discretion of a man deferreth his anger, and it is his glory to pass over a transgression." Also, another one said, "This one thing, as being a scandal, is to be much guarded against, namely, that if the sub-prior be removed, henceforward learned clerks will not deign to take on them the religious habit in our house, if it should happen that any dumb image be set up, and a wooden log be preferred in such a convent as ours." And the same brother added somewhat more, saying that a person to be prior of our convent, should be such a one that if any question of great importance arose in the abbot's absence concerning ecclesiastical or secular affairs, it might be referred to the prior, as being the highest and most discreet person.

A certain one of our brethren, hearing these and such like things, said, "What good is it that ye multiply so many and such sayings? When the abbot comes home, he will do as he pleases about it. Perhaps he may seek the advice of each of us singly, and with great show of formality; but in the end, by allegations and by plausible reasonings and circumlocutions, he will at last come down to the fulfilment of his own desire; and the affair will end as he has all along intended."

The abbot, therefore, having returned, and sitting in chapter, set forth to us amply and eloquently enough what sort of man ought to be appointed prior. John the third prior answered, in the presence of us all, that the sub-prior was a worthy and fit person. But the greater number immediately opposed, saying, "A man of peace, let a man of peace be given us." Two of us, therefore, replied to them, saying that a person should be appointed who knew how to direct the souls of men, and to distinguish "between leprosy and leprosy," which saying gave great offence, for it seemed to favour the part of the sub-prior. But the abbot hearing this uproar, said that he would after chapter hear what each had to say, and so proceed advisedly in the business, and upon the morrow would dispatch it as he thought fit.

In the meantime some one said that the abbot would go through this formality in order that the sub-prior should be cautiously shelved from the office of prior, as if it had been done by the advice of the convent, not by the desire of the abbot; and so he, the abbot, would be held excused, and by this policy the mouth of them that speak lies should be stopped.

On the morrow the abbot, as he sat in chapter, wept sorely, saying that he had passed the whole night without sleep, for sheer anxiety and apprehension that he might chance to nominate one who was displeasing to God. He swore upon peril of his soul that he would nominate four of us who, according to his opinion, were most serviceable and fit, so that we should choose one from those four. Therefore the abbot, in the first place, named the sacrist, whom he well knew to be infirm and insufficient, as the sacrist himself testified with an oath. Forthwith, in the presence of all, he named John the third prior, his cousin, and Maurice his chaplain, and the before-named Herbert, all indeed young men, of about forty years old or under, and all of them of moderate learning, and, so far as respects the cure of souls, rather requiring to be taught than learned therein, nevertheless apt to learn.

These three the abbot nominated and preferred, passing over the sub-prior, and passing by many others of the seniors and elders, experienced and learned men, some who had formerly been masters of the schools, as well as all others. The abbot dwelt long in speaking of and commending the person of John in many respects; but, nevertheless, on the other side, alleged that the great number of his relations in this province would lie heavy on his neck if he were prior.

Now, when the abbot was about to allege the same thing concerning Maurice (and he could with reason do it), so that in a roundabout way he should come to make mention of Herbert, his discourse was interrupted by one of the elders of the convent saying, "Master precentor, you have the first voice; name Master Herbert." "He is a good man," said he. On hearing the name of Herbert, the abbot stopped speaking, and turning to the precentor, said, "I have no objection to receive Herbert if you will." On this saying, the whole convent cried out, "He is a good man; he is a good and amiable man"; and this same thing also many of the elders testified. Immediately hereupon the precentor and some one in alliance with him, and two others on the other side, arose with all haste, and put Herbert in the midst.

Herbert, indeed, at first humbly begged to be excused, saying that he was insufficient to fill such a dignity, and particularly, as he said, he was not of such perfect knowledge that he should know how to make a sermon in chapter in such manner as would become a prior. Most of those who witnessed this were amazed, and for very confusion struck dumb. However, the abbot said in answer many things to re-assure him, and as it were in disparagement of learned men, saying that he could well remember and con over the sermons of others, just as others did; and began to condemn rhetorical flourishes, and pompous words, and choice sentences, saying that in many churches the sermon in convent is delivered in French, or rather in English, for moral edification, not for literary ostentation.

After this had been said, the new prior advanced to the feet of the abbot and kissed them. The abbot received him with tears, and with his own hand placed him in the prior's seat, and commanded all that they should pay him the reverence and obedience due to him as prior.

The chapter being over, I being hospitaller, sat in the porch of the guest-hall, stupefied, and revolving in my mind the things I had heard and seen; and I began to consider closely for what cause and for what particular merits such a man should be advanced to so high a dignity. And I began to reflect that the man was of comely stature and of striking appearance; handsome and pleasant looking; always cheerful; of a smiling countenance, be it early or late; kind to all; a man calm in his bearing, and grave in his gait; polite in speech, possessing a sweet voice in chanting, and expressive in reading; young, strong, of a healthy body, and always in readiness to undergo travail for the needs of the church; skilful in conforming himself to every circumstance of place or time, either with ecclesiastics, clerks or seculars; liberal and social, and gentle in reproof; not spiteful, not suspicious, not covetous, not tiresome, not slothful; sober and fluent of tongue in the French idiom, as being a Norman by birth; a man of moderate understanding, who, if "too much learning should make him mad," might be said to be a perfectly accomplished man.

When I regarded these things I said in my mind, such a man would become very popular, but "there is nothing every way blessed," and I wept for joy, saying that "God hath visited his people; as the Lord pleased, so it hath been done." But of a sudden another thought occurred to me: "Be cautious in your praise of a new man, for honours alter manners, or rather they show them. Wait and see who and what sort of men will be his counsellors, and to whom he will give ear, for each thing naturally draws to its like. The event will prove his doings, and therefore be sparing in your praises."

On the same day certain unlearned brethren, as well officials as cloister-folk, came together, and "whetted their tongues like a sword that they might shoot privily at" the learned, repeating the words of the abbot, which he had that day spoken, as it were to the prejudice of the learned. Thus they said to one another, "Now let our philosophers take to their philosophies: now is it manifest what their philosophies are worth. So often have our good clerks declined in the cloister that they are now declined. So much have they sermonized in chapter that all are driven away. So much have they spoken of discerning between leprosy and leprosy that as lepers they are all put out. So often have they declined *musa, musae*, that all of them are reckoned musards" (drivellers). These and such like things certain uttered in ridicule and scandal of others, justifying their own ignorance: they condemned the knowledge of polite learning, and disparaged learned men, being very merry, and expecting great things, which, in all probability, will never come to pass, for "Hope of good is often deceived in its expectation."

CHAPTER XVII
THE ABBOT'S FOIBLES

THE wise man hath said, "No one is in every respect perfect"; nor was the abbot Samson. For this reason let me say this, that according to my judgment the abbot was not to be commended when he caused a deed to be made and ordered the same to be delivered to a certain servant of his, for him to have the sergeanty of John Ruffus, after the decease of the same John. Ten marks, as it was said, "did blind the eyes of the wise." Wherefore, upon Master Dennis, the monk, saying that such an act was unheard of, the abbot replied: "I shall not cease from doing as I like a whit the more for you than I would for that youngster." The abbot also did the like thing in respect of the sergeanty of Adam the infirmarer, upon payment of one hundred shillings. Of such an act it may be said, "A little leaven leaveneth the whole lump."

There is, also, another stain of evil doing, which I trust in the Lord he will wash away with tears, in order that a single excess may not disfigure the sum total of so many good deeds. He built up the bank of the fish-pond at Babwell so high, for the service of a new mill, that by the keeping back of the water there is not a man, rich or poor, who has land near the water, from the gate of the town to Eastgate, but has lost his garden and his orchards. The pasture of the cellarer, upon the other side of the bank, is spoilt. The arable land, also, of the neighbouring folk has been much deteriorated. The meadow of the cellarer is ruined, the orchard of the infirmarer has been flooded by the great flow of water, and all the neighbouring folk are complaining thereof. Once, indeed, the cellarer argued with him in full chapter, upon this excessive damage; but he, quickly moved to anger, made answer, that his fish-pond was not to be spoilt on account of our meadows.

The Dean of London writes thus in his chronicles: "King Henry the Second, having conferred with the archbishop and bishops concerning the vacant abbacies, so far observed the rule of the canons in appointing abbots, that it was the custom to appoint them upon votes solicited from other houses; thinking, perhaps, that if pastors were set up in every place from their own body," a previously contracted familiarity would afford impunity to vice, and old acquaintanceship would give indulgence to wickedness, and thereby too great remissness would obtain in cloisters. Another has said: "It does not seem fit that a pastor should be elected from his own house, but rather from some other house; because, if he is taken from elsewhere he will always believe, according to the greatness of the monastery which he has undertaken to rule, that many are good men and true, whose advice he will seek if he is a good man, and whose honesty he will fear if he is a bad one. But a servant of the house, better knowing the ignorance, inability and incompetence of every one, will the more carelessly serve therein, mixing square with round."

The monks of Ramsey followed this line of reasoning; for in those days, when they were able to choose one of their own body, on two occasions they chose an abbot from other houses.

In the year of grace one thousand two hundred and one there came to us the abbot of Flay, and through his preaching caused the open buying and selling which took place in the market on Sundays to be done away with, and it was ordained that the market should be held on the Monday. The like the abbot brought to pass in many cities and boroughs of England.

In the same year the monks of Ely set up a market at Lakenheath, having the permission, as well as the charter, of the King. Now, we in the first place, dealing peaceably with our friends and neighbours, sent our messengers to the chapter of Ely, and, first of all, to the lord Bishop of Ely, letters of request that he should forbear his intentions; adding that we could, in a friendly way, for the sake of peace and preserving our mutual regard, pay the fifteen marks that were given as a fine for obtaining the King's charter. Why make a long story of it? They would not give way, and then upon all sides arose threatening speeches, and "spears threatening spears."

We therefore procured a writ of inquest to ascertain whether that market was established to our prejudice, and to the damage of the market of the town of St. Edmund. The oath was made, and it was testified that this had been done to our damage. Of all which, when the King was informed, he caused it to be inquired, by his registrar, what sort of charter he had granted to the monks of Ely; and it was made to appear that he had given to them the aforesaid market, under such conditions that it should not be to the injury of the neighbouring markets. The King, therefore, forty marks being offered, granted us his charter that from thenceforward there should be no market within the liberty of St. Edmund, unless by the assent of the abbot. And he wrote to Geoffrey Fitz-Peter, his justiciary, that the market of Lakenheath should be abolished. The justiciary wrote the same to the sheriff of Suffolk.

The sheriff, being well aware that he could not enter upon the liberties of St. Edmund, or exercise any authority there, gave it in charge to the abbot, by his writ, that this should be performed according to the form of the royal command. The steward of the hundred, therefore, coming thither upon the market day, with the witnessing of freemen, in the King's name openly prohibited that market, showing the letters of the King and the sheriff; but being treated with great abuse and violence, he departed, without having accomplished his object.

The abbot, on the other hand, deferring this matter for awhile, being at London, and consulting the learned thereupon, commanded his bailiffs, that taking with them the men of St. Edmund with horse and arms, they should abolish the market, and that they should bring along with them in custody the buyers and sellers therein, if they should find any. So at dead of night, there went forth nearly six hundred men well armed, proceeding towards Lakenheath. But when the scouts gave intelligence of their arrival, all who were in the market ran hither and thither, and not one of them could be found.

Now, the prior of Ely on that same night had come thither, with his bailiffs, expecting the arrival of our men, in order that, to the best of his ability, he might defend the buyers and sellers; but he would not stir out of his inn. When our bailiffs had required from him gage and pledge to stand trial in the court of St. Edmund for the wrong committed by him, and he had refused, upon consultation, they overturned the butchers' shambles and the tables of the stalls in the market, and carried them away with them. Moreover, they led away with them all the cattle, "all sheep and oxen; yea, and the beasts of the field," and set off towards Icklingham. The bailiffs of the prior following them made suit for their cattle, by replevin within fifteen days: and their suit was allowed. Within the fifteen days there came a writ, whereby the abbot was summoned to come before the court of exchequer to answer for such act, and that the cattle taken should in the meantime be delivered up without charge. For the Bishop of Ely, who was an eloquent and well-spoken man, in his own person had made complaint thereof to the justiciary and the nobles of England, saying that a most unheard-of piece of arrogance had been committed in the land of St. Etheldreda in time of peace; wherefore many were highly indignant with the abbot.

In the meanwhile another cause of disagreement arose between the bishop and the abbot. A certain young man of Glemsford had been summoned to the court of St. Edmund, for a breach of the King's peace, and had been sought for a long while. At length the steward of the bishop brought forth that young man in the county court, claiming the jurisdiction of the court of St. Etheldreda, and exhibiting the charters and privileges of his lord; but our bailiffs, claiming the jurisdiction of the plaint and the seisin of such liberty, could not be heard. The county court, indeed, put that plaint in respite until the justices in eyre should arrive, wherefore St. Edmund was ousted of his jurisdiction. The abbot, on hearing this, proposed to go over to the King; but because he was sick, he decided to defer the matter till the Purification.

And, behold! on St. Agnes day there came the King's messenger, bearing the writ of our lord the Pope, wherein it was contained, that the bishop of Ely and the abbot of St. Edmund should make inquisition concerning

Geoffrey Fitz-Peter and William de Stutville, and certain other lords of England who had taken the cross, for whom the King required discharge, alleging their personal infirmity, and the necessity for their advice in the government of his kingdom. The same messenger also brought letters from our lord the King, commanding that he, upon the sight thereof, should come to him to confer upon the message of our lord the Pope. The abbot was troubled in his mind, and said, "I am straitened on every side; I must either offend God or the King: by the very God, whatsoever may be the consequence to me, I will not wittingly lie."

Therefore, returning home with all speed, somewhat weakened by infirmity of body and humbled, and (as was not his wont) timid, by the intervention of the prior, he sought advice of us (a thing he heretofore had seldom done), as to what course he was to pursue in respect of the liberties of the church which were in jeopardy, and whence the money was to come if he took his journey, and to whom the keeping of the abbey was to be committed, and what should be done for his poor servants who had a long time served him. And the answer was, that he might go, and that he was at liberty to take up at interest sufficient money, to be payable out of our sacristy and from our pittances, and from our other rents at his pleasure; and that he should give the abbey in charge to the prior, and some other clerk whom he had enriched, and who could, in the interval, live upon his own means, that thereby a saving might take place in the expenses of the abbot, and that he might give to each of his servants money proportioned to his length of service.

He, hearing such counsel, was pleased therewith, and so it was done. The abbot, therefore, coming into chapter the day before he took his departure, caused to be brought with him all his books, and these he presented to the church and convent, and commended our counsel which we had signified to him through the prior.

In the meantime we heard certain persons murmuring, saying that the abbot is careful and solicitous for the liberties of his own barony, but he keeps silence respecting the liberties of the convent which we have lost in his time; namely, concerning the lost court and liberties of the cellarer, and the liberty of the sacrist, as regards the appointment of the bailiffs of the town by the convent. Therefore, the Lord raised up the spirit of three brethren of but indifferent knowledge, who, having got many others to join them, conferred with the prior thereupon, in order that he should speak with the abbot respecting these matters. On our behalf the prior was to ask him, at his departure, to provide for the security of his church in respect of those liberties. On hearing this, the abbot answered that no more was to be said upon the subject, swearing that so long as he lived he would be the master; but towards evening he talked more mildly thereupon with the prior.

On the morrow, indeed, sitting in chapter, as he was about to depart and ask licence so to do, he said he had satisfied all his servants, and had made his will just as if he was now to die; and beginning to speak concerning those liberties, he justified himself, saying that he had changed the ancient customs in order that there should not be a default in the administration of the King's justice, and threw the blame upon the sacrist, and said that if Durand, the town bailiff, who was now sick, should die, the sacrist might hold the bailiwick in his own hand, and present a bailiff to the chapter for approval, as the custom had been of old, so nevertheless that this be done with the assent of the abbot; but the gifts and offerings to be made yearly by the bailiff he would in no wise remit.

Now, when we asked him what was to be done in respect of the cellarer's court which was lost, and especially of the halfpence which the cellarer was accustomed to receive for renewing pledges, he became angry, and asked us in his turn by what authority we demanded the exercise of regal jurisdiction, and those things which appertain to regalities.

To this it was replied that we had possessed it from the foundation of the church, and even three years after he had come to the abbacy, and this liberty of renewing pledges we possessed in every one of our manors. We stated that we ought not to lose our right in consideration of a hundred shillings, which he received privately from the town bailiff every year; and we boldly required of him to give us such seisin thereof as we had had even in his time.

The abbot, being as it were at a loss for an answer, and willing enough to leave us all in peace and to depart quietly, ordered that those halfpence and the other matters which the cellarer demanded should be sequestrated until his return; and he promised that upon his return he would co-operate with us in everything, and make just order and disposition, and render to each what was justly his. On his saying this, all was quiet again; but the calm was not very great, for

"In promises any man may wealthy be."

FINIS.

APPENDICES:

APPENDIX I
SAMSON AS AN AUTHOR.

SAMSON having been generally looked upon as a man of action rather than as a man of letters, it seems desirable to consider at greater length than is possible in the general Introduction, his claims to be regarded as a literary character.

In the Bodleian Library at Oxford is a huge codex of 898 pages (MS. 240) in a script of the 14th century. This once belonged to Bury Abbey, as at the beginning is the note "Liber monachorum Sancti Edmundi, in quo continetur secunda pars Historia auree, quam scribi fecit dominus Rogerus de Huntedoun sumptibus graciarum suarum anno domini MCCC.LXXVII°." Over the title is written on the margin "Thomas Prise possidet," and in another hand "Io. Anglicus erat author."

There is considerable difficulty in assigning the exact authorship of this work: but that it was compiled at Bury is certain, and it was no doubt added to as new materials turned up or were deemed worthy of admission, especially such as were connected with St. Edmundsbury. Dr. Carl Horstman has published in the preface to Vol. I. of his *Nova Legenda Anglie* (Oxf. Univ. Press, 1901) a summary of the contents of this book which throws much new light on its *provenance*. It is, as he says, "the depository of documents of Bury Abbey, and not the work of one individual; but the joint work, the common concern of the monastery, for a whole generation."

The MS. contains only the second part of the Historia aurea, and with an abbreviated text; and this is followed by a collection of miscellanies, lives of saints, poetry and documents of all sorts. Dr. Horstman prints in his second volume the lives of several saints, scattered through the last half of the codex.

The only one of these lives that need concern us is that of St. Edmund, which is very long and detailed, and occupies 116 printed pages. This is followed almost immediately by a chapter De modo meditandi vel contemplandi (including St. Edmund's prayer, "Gratias tibi ago"), and later by a compilation on monastic discipline for the novices of Bury Abbey.

This Life of St. Edmund is by far the most complete extant. It is described as "Vita et passio cum miraculis sancti Edmundi regis et martiris, excerpta de cronicis et diuersis historiis seu legendis, de eodem breuiter et sub compendio compilata." It is doubtless the "Prolixa vita" from which was compiled the "abbreviata vita" included in Abbot Curteys' Register (now at the British Museum), and printed in Archdeacon Battely's book of 1745 (pp.

25, 149). In the margins are given the authorities from which it is compiled, and amongst these are, in addition to the chronicles of Blythburgh, Ely, Hoveden, Hulme, Huntingdon, Malmesbury, Marianus, Norwich, Sarum, Waringford, and Westminster, the writers specially identified with Bury Abbey:—Abbo of Fleury, Herman the Archdeacon, Galfridus de Fontibus, Osbert of Clare, Jocelin of Brakelond (from whom are taken the incidents described in chapters viii. and xiv. of this book), and—Samson.

There are in all eighteen sections of the Life for which Samson is quoted as the authority. On eight occasions the word "Sampson" appears in the margin; "Sampson abbas," eight times; "Sampson abbas sancti Edmundi," once; "Ex libro de miraculis eius Sampson," once (the first occasion when the name appears); and "Ex libro primo miraculorum Sampson abb." once (the seventh occasion).

Before considering Samson's share in the collection of materials relative to the history of St. Edmund, a few words must be said about the earlier writers on the subject.

The first contributor to the tangle of legends and miracles connected with St. Edmund and his shrine was ABBO, of Fleury, a great monastery on the Loire above Orleans, founded in the 7th century. A native of Orleans, Abbo was sent early to the monastic school at Fleury, where he mastered five of the seven arts, viz., grammar, arithmetic, dialectic, astronomy and music. (Migne's *Patrologia*, vol. 139.) A deputation coming to Fleury from the monks of Ramsey Abbey, asking that a man of learning might be sent to them, Abbo was selected for the office, and he remained two years in England, when he was recalled. He died from a spear-thrust in November, 1004. Whilst in England (circa 985) he heard from Archbishop Dunstan the story of St. Edmund's death, as related to Dunstan when a youth by an old man who said he was armour-bearer to St. Edmund on the day of his death (20th November, 870). At the entreaty of the monks of Ramsey, Abbo put this story into writing, prefacing it with a dedicatory epistle to Dunstan in which he says that the work is sent to the Archbishop because every part of it, except the last miracle, is related on his authority.

Abbo being "composition master" to the student monks at Ramsey, he wrote, as Mr. Arnold says (I. xiv.), "with that freedom with which men whose information is scanty, and their imagination strong, are not sorry to enjoy." Lord Francis Hervey, in a masterly analysis of the facts and fictions of St. Edmund's life in his Notes to Robert Reyce's *Breviary of Suffolk* (1902), thus sums the matter with great truth: "Abbo's treatise, with its declamatory flourishes and classical tags, is for historical purposes all but worthless."

The copies extant of Abbo's *Passio* are numerous. (For List, see Hardy's Catalogue, vol. i, p. 526.) At least four of them (two in the Cottonian collection, one at the Bodleian, and one at Lambeth) belonged to Bury Abbey, the earliest being Tiberius B. ii., which has on fol. 1*a* the words "Liber feretrariorum S. Edmundi in quo continentur uita passio et miracula S. Edmundi." It is a beautiful MS. of the end of the eleventh or beginning of the twelfth century; "and the gold enrichment is sometimes splendid" (Arnold I. lxv.), though the illumination is unfinished. The other Cottonian MS. (Titus A. viii.) is of the thirteenth century, and has on fol. 65 the words "Liber monachorum S. Edmundi." (Both these books will be referred to later.)

The next writer on the subject was HERMAN THE ARCHDEACON, who, at the end of the eleventh century, wrote a treatise *De Miraculis Sancti Eadmundi*.

Herman was Archdeacon to Bishop Arfast of Thetford, at the time when the latter first endeavoured to establish his see at Bury; but later he must have become a monk of St. Edmund, and he manifests in his narrative enthusiastic devotion to the monastery. In the prologue he explains that he compiled his work at the request of Abbot Baldwin "felicis memoriæ" (died 1097), partly from oral tradition, partly from an old and almost undecipherable manuscript "exarata calamo cujusdam difficillimo, et, ut ita dicam, adamantino." Mr. Arnold has printed the text of Herman on pp. 26-92 of his vol. I. from the Cottonian volume Tiberius B. ii. above referred to, which is composed of Abbo's *Passio* and Herman's *Miracula*.

A third writer was GALFRIDUS DE FONTIBUS, who wrote in the days of Abbot Ording (1146-1156) a short tract, *De Infantia Sancti Eadmundi*, of which only one MS. is known (in the Cambridge University Library). Further additions to the legends and miracles were made by OSBERT of CLARE, prior of Westminster, who flourished between 1108 and 1140, but whose writings are not now separately extant, though extracts from them appear in the manuscripts of other authors.

It would seem that working upon all these records, and doubtless others which have not descended to us, Samson, at the period of his life when he was still a subordinate officer of Bury Abbey, set about compiling a treatise of his own. His prologue indicates that he was moved to narrate the glorious miracles of the glorious king and martyr St. Edmund by the orders of his superiors and the exhortations of his fellow monks. His work seems, however, to have been mainly that of a compiler and editor, though the prologue, described by Mr. Arnold (I., liii.) as "written in a massive and manly style," was doubtless of his own composition. The work appears after Abbo's *Passio* in the Cottonian MS. Titus A. viii., and consists of two books, Liber I. containing sixteen chapters, and Liber II. twenty-one chapters. All but four of the chapters in the first book refer to narratives that had been told before by Herman, and Samson "has merely re-written them, adding no new facts, but greatly improving the style." The second book contains another prologue, followed by a prefatory letter; and a hand of the fourteenth or early fifteenth century has written in the Cottonian MS. "Osberti de Clara prioris Westmonasterii" in the margin of the prologue, and "Incipit epistola Osberti prioris Westmonasterii missa con. S. Edmundi de miraculis ejusdem" in the margin at the beginning of the letter.

Mr. Arnold speaks of the "inflated diction and fantastical mystical interpretations" of this (second) prologue and prefatory letter, and says that "Samson seems simply to have annexed them while making up his own work." As, however, some of the narratives in this second book are ascribed to Samson himself in the Bodleian MS. 240, whilst others in the same book are ascribed to Osbert, it is manifest that some confusion had arisen in the interval as to the respective shares of responsibility for the narratives. But this need not prevent us from accepting Samson as at least the compiler and editor of the work *De Miraculis Sancti Edmundi* referred to on page xxxiv. of the Introduction, and printed in full on pp. 107-208 of Mr. Arnold's first volume.

If it be the case, as Mr. Arnold thinks (and there seems no reason against the ascription) that the Prologue of Book I. was Samson's own composition, it will doubtless be of interest that it should be reproduced here as a specimen of his literary style; and a translation of it is therefore subjoined, which follows the structure of the original as closely as possible:—

"When we see the deeds of many earthly men extolled in brilliant writings, which those skilled in letters have handed down to the memory of posterity, it is to be wondered that we do not blush that the great works of God, which, through His servants, have been brought into being almost in this our very age, should through our sloth be blotted out, and through our silence be condemned. And although those secular historians, in the pride of their eloquence, have said very much about small affairs, and have gained the favour and tickled the ears of their audience by the sweetness of their speech, yet Christian simplicity and Catholic plainness, innocent of the leaven of superstition, are rightly preferred to them all. Indeed, the greatest faith is to be placed in the account of those who do not wish, and do not know how, to colour what they have heard, or, by the grace of their words, to twist matters into one tortuous path after another.

"In saying this we do not impudently speak to the discredit (be that far from us) of Churchmen who, by the divine inspiration, endowed with wonderful eloquence, have with their words, sweeter than honey and the honeycomb, adorned the deeds of our honoured ancestors, as it were a golden tablet ornamented with most brilliant pearls. But verily those are to be confuted who are carried headlong by a damnable presumption to that with which erudition has nought to do, and to which the grace of the Holy Spirit imparts nought.

"But we (whom the apostle warns lest we should despise the riches of the goodness of God, and whom he exhorts not to receive His grace in vain) with a truthful, albeit an unpolished style, at the command of superior authority and by the exhortation of brotherly love, have undertaken to tell of the glorious miracles of the glorious king and martyr Edmund: since, indeed, it appears impious that we should allow the lantern, which God lighted and placed upon a candlestick, to be obscured through our sloth, or should hide it negligently under the bushel of oblivion. For to this purpose is it placed upon a candlestick, that it may give light to all who are in the house."

In which matter the victorious champion of God, Edmund, illuminating the borders, not only of Britain, but also of foreign lands with the glory of his miracles, gives frequent token of his merit towards God.

"On behalf of whose merits, Omnipotent God, we pray That Thou in Thy clemency wouldst purge our inmost heart, And wouldst infuse the gift which the fostering spirit bestows, Opening the tongues of speechless babes and making them eloquent, That we may be able worthily to tell the praises of the martyr, His famous acts, his virtues and his triumphs."

APPENDIX II
NOTES TO THE TEXT OF THE CHRONICLE.

[The full titles of the works of reference quoted in the pages of this Appendix as "Arnold," "Battely," "James," "Rokewode," will be found on pages 276 and 277 of Appendix III].

CHAPTER I.

1, 4. *The year when the Flemings were taken captive.* On the 17th October, 1173, Richard de Lucy, the chief justiciary of King Henry II., defeated at Fornham St. Genevieve, near Bury St. Edmunds, the rebel Robert de Beaumont, Earl of Leicester, who had landed from Flanders at Walton in Suffolk on the 29th September, 1173, at the head of a force of Flemings. The chroniclers speak of large numbers of the foreign mercenaries as being killed at the battle of Fornham. The Earl and Countess of Leicester were captured, and imprisoned at Falaise till 1174. For an interesting description of the battle, with many references to the chronicles, see Miss Kate Norgate's *England under the Angevin Kings*, II. 150-1.

1, 10. *Hugh the Abbot.* Hugh, Prior of Westminster, succeeded Ording as 9th Abbot of St. Edmundsbury in 1157. Gervase records his being blessed by Archbishop Theobald at Colchester, and his vowing to him canonical obedience. But a bull obtained at great cost from Pope Alexander III. in 1172 (see p. 7) made the abbey immediately subject to Rome. Some details of the occurrences during his abbacy are given in Battely, pp. 78-82.

1, 11. Genesis xxvii. 1.

2, 21. *Debt ... to Jews.* Whilst the Jews were legally simply chattels of the king, they were at this time "practically masters of the worldly interests of a large number of his Christian subjects, and of a large portion of the wealth of his realm" (Norgate's *Angevin Kings*, II. 487). There are many instances besides that of St. Edmundsbury of ecclesiastical property and furniture being pledged to the Jews, *e.g.* the sacred vessels and jewels of Lincoln Minster were in pledge to Aaron, a rich Jew of that city, for seven years or more before Geoffrey, bishop-elect, redeemed them in 1173.

3, 6. *Benedict the Jew.* In 1171 "Benedict the Jew, son of Deodate, was fined xx^{li} for taking certain sacred vestments in pawn." (Pipe Rolls, Norf. and Suff. 17 Hen. II.) Other fines on Jews are recorded by Rokewode (pp. 106-7).

3, 9. *William the sacrist.* From the *Gesta Sacristarum* (Arnold II. 291) we learn of this officer, who was once Samson's superior, afterwards a rival candidate for the abbacy, and finally Samson's subordinate, "Huic [Schuch] successit Willelmus cognomento Wiardel; qui non sine causa a domino Samsone abbate amotus fuit ab administratione." His evil deeds recorded by Jocelin appear therefore to have been remembered.

<u>6</u>, 1. *Richard the Archbishop.* Richard was a Norman by birth and of humble parentage; and was prior of Dover when the question of filling up the primacy was discussed 2½ years after Becket's murder on 29th December, 1170. There was a disputed election, but Robert, by the Court influence, won the day over Odo, Prior of Canterbury; and eventually his election was confirmed by Pope Alexander III. on 2nd April, 1174. Immediately after his enthronisation (5th October, 1174) Richard held a legatine visitation of his province; and as he rode with a great train, his visits were specially grievous to the religious houses that had to receive him.

<u>6</u>, 19. *Sent to Acre.* Castleacre, Westacre, and Southacre, in Norfolk, are all described in Domesday book as "Acra." There were two Priories, one at Castleacre, the other at Westacre; but the former was the more famous of the two. As it was a Cluniac institution, and as the Cluniacs were a kind of stricter Benedictines, it seems most probable that it was to Castleacre that Samson was sent as a punishment. Apparently this was his second banishment there; for he speaks here to Jocelin (then a novice, and who joined the monastery in 1173) as though of recent events. (As to his first imprisonment after his return from Rome about 1161, see page 74 and note on p. 237.) The Priory of Castleacre was founded about 1084 by William de Warrenne, created by the Conqueror Earl of Surrey, and the progenitor of that famous sixth Earl who fought Baliol and Wallace in Scotland, and who, when called upon by the King's Commissioners to produce the title by which he held his possessions, drew his sword and laid it on the table. Some remarkably beautiful ruins of the Priory, particularly of its west front and the Prior's Lodge, have happily escaped the ravages of the village builders, who for centuries used the ruins as a stone quarry.

<u>6</u>, 24. Exodus v. 21.

<u>7</u>, 4. *authority as legate.* Mr. Rokewode goes at length (pp. 107-8) into the documents relative to the claim of the monks of St. Edmund to exemption under Royal authority from ordinary episcopal jurisdiction. The Bull of 1172 which they obtained from Pope Alexander III. exempted them from the jurisdiction of any other ecclesiastical authority than the Pontiff or his *legatus a latere.* Shortly afterwards the Monastery was exempted from the personal interference of Archbishop Richard as legate *a latere.*

<u>8</u>, 5. *Jurnet the Jew.* Rokewode quotes (pp. 108-9) from the Pipe Rolls of Henry II. the following: In 23 Henry II., Jurnet the Jew of Norwich was amerced in MM marcs; and he stood amerced, in the 31st year of the same

king, in MMMMMDXXV marcs and a half, for which debt the whole body of Jews were chargeable: and they were to have Jurnet's effects and chattels to enable them to pay it. He gave King Richard MDCCC marcs that he might reside in England with the King's good will.

10, 23. *morrow of St. Brice.* November 15, 1180. Hugh was buried in the Chapter House nearest the door, sixth and last of the six abbots buried there, as recorded in a MS. at Douai circa 1425. The other five were:—Ording (1146-1156), Samson (1182-1211), Richard of Insula (1229-1234), Henry of Rushbrook (1234-1248), Edmund of Walpole (1248-1257). The lidless coffins of these five, with skeletons within, were discovered January 1, 1903. The coffin of Hugh had disappeared, but bones which may have been his were found buried at the spot.

CHAPTER II.

12, 3. *Ranulf de Glanville.* The famous author of the oldest of our legal classics, the "Treatise on the Laws and Customs of England," was of Suffolk stock, and was born at Stratford St. Andrew, Saxmundham. He succeeded Richard Lucy as chief justiciary of England, and thenceforward he was the king's right-hand man (Richard of Devizes called him the "King's eye"). At the moment of Abbot Hugh's death Henry II. was in France (he kept that Christmas at Le Mans), so the monks appreciated the importance of letting Glanville as justiciary know at once the fact of the vacancy. Glanville took the cross, and died at the siege of Acre in 1180.

12, 11. *wardship of the Abbey.* The accounts rendered by the wardens during the abbatial vacancy have been fortunately preserved in the returns which Wimer, the Sheriff of Norfolk and Suffolk, made to the Exchequer for the 27 and 28 Henry II. Mr. Rokewode gives the actual text of them (pp. 110-1). The rental of the Abbot from Michaelmas, 1180, to Michaelmas, 1181, was £326 12s. 4d.: out of which £56 13s. 4d. was paid for corrodies, including £21 for Abbot Hugh's expenses for the six weeks before his death, and £35 for the Archbishop of Trontheim.

14, 2. Deuteronomy xvi. 19.

14, 9. *paintings.* For an interesting discussion as to these paintings, and the subjects of them, see *James,* pp. 130 *et seq.*

14, 11. *building the great tower.* Samson's work as subsacrist in connection with this tower is thus described by James, page 119: "Samson finished one storey in the great tower at the west end. This was a western tower occupying a position similar to that of the western tower at Ely, immediately over the central western door." It was *not* this tower (as stated by Rokewode, page 111) that fell down on 23 Sept., 1210, but the central tower (see James, pp. 121-203).

<u>16</u>, 7. Judges xvi. 19.

<u>16</u>, 11. Judges xvi. 29.

<u>16</u>, 18. Matthew xxv. 21.

<u>17</u>, 7. Quot homines tot sententiæ. Terence, *Phormio*, Act. 2, Sc. 3, 14.

<u>17</u>, 12. *Abbot Ording.* In the dedication to Abbot Ording of the *Liber de Infantia Sancti Eadmundi* by Galfridus de Fontibus, Ording is said (Arnold, i. 93) to have been "watchful in attendance on the King from his boyhood." Apparently this King was Stephen (born about 1097), as Henry II., his successor, was not born until 1133. At that time Ording would have been on duty at Bury: for he was already Prior in 1136, when Anselm, then Abbot, was nominated for the Bishopric of London. Ording was appointed in 1138 Abbot in Anselm's place; but as the latter failed to get his nomination to the See of London confirmed by the Pope, he came back to Bury. Ording therefore, "sive volens sive nolens" had to return to his duties as Prior; but when Anselm died in 1148, Ording was re-elected Abbot, and held office till he died in 1156. As to his place of burial, see note to p. 152, l. 5, on p. 247.

<u>17</u>, 23. Matthew xvi. 19.

<u>18</u>, 9. *Barrators of Norfolk.* Barrator==an incitor to lawsuits (from O. Fr. *bareter*, to deceive, cheat). The men of Norfolk were noted for their litigious propensities (cf. Tusser's rhyming autobiography: "Norfolk wiles, so full of guiles"). Fuller in his *Worthies* says: "Whereas *pedibus ambulando* is accounted but a vexatious suit in other countries, here (where men are said to study law as following the plough-tail) some would persuade us that they will enter an action for their neighbour's horse but looking over their hedge." An Act was passed in 1455 (33 Hen. VI. cap. 7) to check the litigiousness of "the City of Norwich, and the counties of Norfolk and Suffolk."

<u>18</u>, 17. Acts xxvi. 24, 25.

<u>20</u>, 13. 1 Corinthians xiii. 11.

<u>21</u>, 4. Romans xvi. 5.

<u>21</u>, 6. *Blood-letting season* (tempore minutionis). At stated times of the year there was a general blood-letting among the monks; and in the same *Liber Albus* in which Jocelin's chronicle appears is a set of Regulations *De Minutis Sanguine* (fol. 193). Amongst the servants in the infirmary of Bury Monastery was *Minutor, cum garcione* (*id.* fol. 44). The effects of the minutio were supposed to last three days, during which the monk did not go to matins.

<u>21</u>, 17. Nihil est ab omni parte beatum. Horace, *Od.* i. 16.

<u>22</u>, 8. John xix. 22.

<u>22</u>, 9. Et semel emissum volat irrevocable verbum. Horace i. *Ep*. 18. 71.

<u>22</u>, 23. Medio tutissimus ibis. Ovid, *Metamorphoses* ii. 137.

<u>23</u>, 1. Matthew xix. 12.

<u>23</u>, 3. *Archbishop of Norway.* In 1180 Eystein (Augustinus) Archbishop of Trontheim, refusing to crown Sverrir, a successful rebel, who had defeated Magnus, King of Norway, was driven into exile and came to England. (William de Newburgh, iii. 16.) Rokewode (p. 113) shows from the accounts of the Wardens of the Abbey during the vacancy, that the corrodies allowed to the Archbishop amounted in all to £94 10s.

<u>23</u>, 11. *Holy child Robert.* Nothing is known of the circumstances of this boy's death at the hands of the Jews, on 10th June, 1181, or of Jocelin's account of it (line 16), beyond the reference made by Bale in his list of Jocelin's writings to *Vita Roberti Martyris.*

<u>23</u>, 13. Acts v. 12.

CHAPTER III

<u>25</u>, 12. Jeremiah xxiii. 40.

<u>25</u>, 21. Cf. 1 Corinthians xii. 3.

<u>26</u>, 23. *Verba Mea.* The 5th Psalm in the Vulgate begins with these words.

<u>31</u>, 9. *Waltham.* The interview with Henry II. took place at Bishop's Waltham, in Hampshire, on the 21st February, 1182.

<u>31</u>, 15. *Geoffrey the Chancellor.* Geoffrey was a natural son of Henry II.—it is generally stated as by Fair Rosamond, though this is now discredited by the facts adduced in the *Dict. Nat. Biog.* He was successively Bishop of Lincoln (1173), Chancellor (1182), Archbishop of York (1191), and after a violent quarrel with King John, fled the country in 1207, dying in Normandy in 1212.

<u>32</u>, 5. Matthew xix. 30; Mark x. 31.

<u>34</u>, 23. *By the very eyes of God:* "per veros oculos Dei!" This was a favourite oath of Henry II. In a contemporary metrical life of St. Thomas of Canterbury, the King is more than once made to exclaim "Par les oilz Dieu" (Rokewode, p. 115). William II. used to swear by "the holy Face of Lucca"; John by "the teeth of God" (Ramsay, *Angevin Empire* (1903), p. 414).

<u>35</u>, 7. *Miserere mei Deus.* Psalm li.

CHAPTER IV

<u>37</u>, 24. *Threshold of the gate.* Samson alighted at what is now known as the "Norman Tower."

<u>38</u>, 4. *Martyri adhuc.* Rokewode gives on page 115 the text (with the musical notes) of this response, the words of which are: "Martyri adhuc palpitanti, sed Christum confitenti, jussit Inguar caput auferri: sicque Edmundus martyrium consummavit, et ad Deum exultans vadit." In a MS. (Digby 109) now at the Bodleian Library (which contains also a copy of Abbo's *Passio*) this response comes after the 5th lesson of the office of St. Edmund.

<u>39</u>, 23. John vi. 6.

<u>39</u>, 24. *New seal.* A representation of this seal is given as the Frontispiece. It is taken from an instrument in the Archives of Canterbury Cathedral, dated 6 November, 1200, being an award in a dispute between the Archbishop of Canterbury and the Canons of Lambeth, referred by Pope Innocent III. to Hugh, Bishop of Lincoln (for whom Roger, Dean of Lincoln, was substituted), Eustace, Bishop of Ely, and Abbot Samson.

The seal represents Abbot Samson, vested in amice, alb, tunic, dalmatic, chasuble, rationale, and mitre. He holds a crozier in his right hand and a closed book in his left. The mitre is unusually large for the date. The inscription is broken, but in full reads thus: "Sigillum Samsonis Dei Gratia Abbatis Sancti Eadmundi." The counterseal (much smaller) displays the lamb bearing a cross, with the words round the circumference, "Secretum Samsonis Abbatis."

<u>41</u>, 9. *Thomas of Hastings.* Apparently the object of Thomas in introducing thus early his nephew, Henry of Hastings, to the notice of Samson, was to secure a recognition by the new Abbot of the claims of his family to the hereditary stewardship of the Liberty of St. Edmund. By Charter of William I., Lidgate in Suffolk, and Blunham in Bedfordshire (where the church is dedicated to St. Edmund), were given to one Ralph to hold in fee of the Abbot of St. Edmund by the service of Dapifer or Steward. Later, between 1115 and 1119, Abbot Albold granted the lands, with the office held by Ralph, to Maurice of Windsor and his heirs, and this grant was confirmed by King Stephen. Maurice was succeeded by Ralph of Hastings, his nephew, and Ralph by William of Hastings, his nephew; and Henry, on whose behalf the claim of the stewardship was made to Samson, was William's son and heir. The Abbot admitted that his right was indisputable (the original Charters of William I., Abbot Albold, Stephen, and Henry II. [two] are quoted by Rokewode, pp. 118-120). But Samson's point seems to have been that Henry was too young to give personal service as Steward, and therefore "the business was deferred." Rokewode observes (p. 117): "Henry continued a minor in 1188, his office being then filled by Robert of Flamville, who held

it at the time of his being one of the Wardens of the Abbey during the vacancy" (see p. 12). In Reece's *Breviary of Suffolk* (1902) John of Hastings is given as Lord of the Manor of Lidgate in 1315.

CHAPTER V

<u>43</u>, 11. *Enclosed many parks.* At the Abbot's manor at Melford was an old deer park of very ancient foundation. It was called Elmsett or Aelmsethe, or the Great Park, and consisted chiefly of open wood. It was in olden times termed "Magnus Boscus Domini," and in the surveys of Edward I. and Henry VI. it is reckoned both as park and wood, the wood part being in the latter survey 217a. 2r. 34p. The whole was impaled round and stored with deer. (Parker's *Melford*, pp. 310-11).

<u>43</u>, 12. *beasts of chase.* The "Beasts of the Chase" in Angevin days were the buck, doe and fox: the "Beasts of the Forest" were the hart, hind and hare: and the "Beasts and Fowls of the Warren" were the hare, rabbit ("coney"), pheasant and partridge. The fox was coupled with the wolf in Canute's Forest Law, No. 27, as "neither forest beasts nor game." When the fox was made a Beast of the Chase cannot be ascertained with any precision. The same Law No. 27, protected "hares, rabbits and roedeer"; the last are not mentioned in later times. In addition to the animals above named, the otter was hunted— *vide* Patent Rolls of Henry III. of 1221. The badger, polecat or wild cat (*catus*) and marten are specified as beasts which receivers of royal licences might hunt "with their own hounds" in the twelfth and thirteenth centuries. There appears to be no such charter or licence granting leave to hunt "the King's great game" (deer): on the contrary, deer are often specially reserved.

<u>43</u>, 12. *Keeping a huntsman with dogs.* The St. Edmund breed of dogs seems to have been celebrated, as Richard I., when there was a difference between him and Samson as to the wardship of Nesta of Cockfield, wrote to the Abbot in a friendly way, and asked him for some of his dogs (page 148). The hunting dog of old times was probably a light sort of mastiff. Sometimes a breed was more celebrated for speed or for strength or for courage, as in the case of the hounds bred by the abbots of Bury. In the course of time the slighter varieties developed into the greyhound, and the thicker into the mastiff of modern times. Canute's Forest Law 31 forbade possession of "the dog which the English call greihounds" to the lower classes. Henry II.'s Assize of the Forest, given at Woodstock 1184, forbids (Clause 2) any one entering a royal forest with bow, arrows, dogs or greyhounds, save with special warrant. Clause 14 requires the lawing of mastiffs.

The Wardrobe Account of Edward I. for 1299-1300, records payment for maintenance of twelve "*fox dogs.*" These were used to kill foxes in coverts previously netted round, so were not, probably, "running hounds." On April 11, 1279, Edward I. wrote to Charles of Salerno promising to send the harriers asked for by the latter: which seems to indicate that the English harrier had a high reputation at that period.

<u>43</u>, 16. *take part in the sport.* Strutt, in his *Sports and Pastimes,* observes:—"By the game laws of Canute, the dignified clergy were permitted to hunt in the forests belonging to the Crown; and their prerogatives were not abrogated by the Normans. Henry II., displeased at the power and ambition of the ecclesiastics, endeavoured to render these grants of none effect by putting in force (1157) the canon law, which strictly forbade the clergy to spend their time in hunting and hawking." Henry III.'s First Charter of 1217 gave leave to an archbishop, bishop, earl or baron to take two deer while passing through a forest "by view of the forester"; or in the absence of that official the sportsman was to blow a horn on killing.

<u>44</u>, 14. *The Eight Hundreds.* These eight hundreds of Thingoe, Thedwastre, Blackbourn, Bradbourn, Bradmere, Lackford, Risbridge and Babergh, with the half hundred of Cosford (see line 18) constituted the Liberty of St. Edmund, as to which see note on page 238.

<u>44</u>, 15. *Robert of Cockfield.* See note to pp. 86, l. 18, on page 241, and cf. pages 254-6.

<u>44</u>, 24. *Hidages, foddercorn, hen-rents.* Hidage was a tax upon every hide of land; foddercorn an ancient feudal right that the lord should be provided with fodder for his horses; hen-rents were a common reservation upon inferior tenures.

<u>45</u>, 11. *Kalendar.* A transcript of this kalendar, which, as stated in the text (p. 45, l. 2) was completed by 1186, is now in the possession of Prince Frederick Dhuleep Singh. In the *History of the Hundred of Thingoe* (1838) an extract from it relating to that Hundred is given on pp. xii.-xvii.

<u>46</u>, 1. *Hugh the subsacrist.* Jocelin says that Samson appointed Hugh subsacrist to William Wiardel, and shortly after (p. 47) made Samson the precentor sacrist. But this arrangement was probably short-lived, for the *Gesta Sacristarum* (Arnold, ii. 290) says Hugh succeeded William as sacrist, and gives a lengthy list of the works he carried out in the church. In 1198, when the body of St. Edmund was examined, Hugh was present, and is described as sacrist (see p. 172).

<u>50</u>, 16. Omnia Cæsar erat. Lucan, *Pharsalia,* iii. 108.

<u>52</u>, 5. Summa petit livor. Ovid, *Remedia Amoris,* 369.

<u>52</u>, 8. 1 John iv. 1.

<u>52</u>, 18. James ii. 13.

<u>54</u>, 9. *School of Melun* (Meludinensium). John of Salisbury calls a scholar of Melun "Meludensis." Peter Abelard opened there, early in the twelfth century, a celebrated school for teaching Dialectic.

<u>54</u>, 23. Ecclesiasticus vii. 24.

<u>57</u>, 14. Strangulat inclusus dolor atque exæstuat intus. Ovid, *Tristia*, v. i. 63.

CHAPTER VI

<u>62</u>, 7. *Pulpit.* This pulpit, from which Samson preached in his native dialect of Norfolk, was one of the works of Hugo the sacrist (Arnold, ii. 291).

<u>65</u>, 3. *Norfolk Barrator.* See note to p. 18, line 9 (pages 226-7).

<u>66</u>, 21. *Sale of holy water.* Ducange cites the acts of a synod of Exeter in 1287, that from ancient times the profits arising from the distribution of holy water had been set apart to maintain poor clerks in schools.

<u>68</u>, 23. *Schools.* Samson is usually credited with having founded a town school in connection with the monastery. This may very likely have been the case, but I have found no direct evidence of it. It seems from this passage that at any rate he provided free lodgings for poor scholars, and from p. 144 that he endowed the mastership of the schools with half the tithes of Wetherden. There is a street at Bury St. Edmunds, just outside the precincts of the monastery, known as School Hall Street.

<u>69</u>, 3. *Manor of Mildenhall.* Edward the Confessor gave Mildenhall to St. Edmund's, but when Domesday Book was compiled it was in the hands of the Crown, being then worth £70. Amongst the Crown lands sold by Richard I. immediately after his accession was this manor, purchased, according to Jocelin, for 1,100 marks, of which 1,000 marks apparently went to the King, and 100 marks to Queen Eleanor (see p. 71, l. 3). See also note to p. 72, l. 4, on page 235.

<u>69</u>, 5. *Expulsion of the Jews.* Arnold (i. 249) expresses the opinion that, "under the circumstances, this must have been the most humane course in the interests of the Jews themselves. All large English towns at this time were imperfectly policed, and the temper of the populace savage and uncertain. A riot having once been set on foot, the only hope of safety for the Jews was in taking refuge in some royal castle. There was no castle at Bury; to the Abbot alone could the survivors [from the massacre in 1190] look for protection; and Samson knew that he had not sufficient force at his command to ensure it to them."

<u>69</u>, 6. *New hospital at Babwell.* The ruins of this hospital, dedicated to the Saviour, still exist in Northgate, beyond the railway arch. It was originally

founded for a warden, twelve chaplains, six clerks, twelve poor gentlemen, and twelve poor women, and was the subject of numerous Charters, which will be found fully described in Chapter II. of the late Sir Wm. Parker's *History of Long Melford* (1873). In the Feet of Fines for Suffolk, 1 John (1199), there are references to two deeds entered into by "Walter, Master of the Hospital of the Blessed Saviour outside the northern gate of St. Edmund's." The Master of the Hospital had his manor at Melford and held his courts: which manor remains to the present day, as the *Manor of the Monks in Melford*. It was at St. Saviour's Hospital that Humphrey, Duke of Gloucester, put up when he was arrested, in February, 1447, by Henry VI., who was in the town for the Parliament which met in the refectory of Bury Abbey.

_70_, 9. *Great roll of Winchester.* Domesday Book: the returns forming the basis of which were transmitted to a board sitting at Winchester, by whom they were arranged in order and placed upon record (Lingard, i. 249).

_70_, 19. *Custom of the realm.* This custom is described by Blackstone (*Commentaries* [1844 ed.] i. 229) as an ancient perquisite called queen-gold or aurum reginæ, due, in the proportion of 10 per cent., from every person making a voluntary offering to the King.

_71_, 1. *Ransom of King Richard.* Richard wrote to his mother from Haguenau on the 19th April, 1193, a letter notifying the 70,000 marks demanded for his ransom by the German Emperor Henry VI. To meet this, the monasteries of England handed over all their gold and silver to royal commissioners, and amongst the treasure delivered up by St. Edmund's was the golden chalice given to the Abbey by Henry II. Queen Eleanor's release of it is printed in the *Monasticon* (1821 ed.), iii. 154 (see also p. 146 of the *Chronicle*).

_71_, 19. *Icklingham.* This appears to be the transaction referred to in a Charter of 1200, granted by Samson (confirmed by King John 15th March, 1200):—"We further give and grant to the said Hospital of St. Saviour, for the maintenance of the poor folk, £12 in money from our town of Icklingham, to be annually received through our sacrist." The signatures to this Charter (given in Parker's *Melford*, p. 9) are interesting. They include "Herbert, the prior," "Hermer, the sub-prior" (see chapter xvi. of this book), and "Jocelin, the almoner" (our Chronicler).

_72_, 4. *confirmed by the King's Charter.* Richard I. signed at Chateau Galliard on 18th July, 1198, two charters (1) confirming to Abbot Samson the manor and advowson of Mildenhall; (2) placing the manor, except Icklingham, at the disposal of the sacrist on certain conditions. At the accession of King John, Samson gave the King £200 for a confirmation of the first Charter, and especially of Mildenhall (cf. Rokewode, pp. 124-5).

<u>72</u>, 15. *Walter of Coutances.* The Church at Woolpit was the first piece of preferment of this famous Archbishop. Walter apparently succeeded, at Woolpit, Geoffrey Ridel, made Bishop of Ely in 1173 (see note on page 237). Rokewode says (p. 126): "Henry II. obtained from Hugh, Abbot of St. Edmund's, in free alms, the Church of Woolpit for his clerk, Walter de Coutances, and in consideration thereof, by charter dated at Winchester, granted that after the decease of Walter or his resignation, the Church should be appropriated to the use of the sick monks" (*Reg. Nigr.* fol. 104 v.). Walter obtained several other appointments, but seems from the text to have retained the Church at Woolpit till 1183, when he was consecrated Bishop of Lincoln. Next year (1184) he was elected Archbishop of Rouen. He took a prominent part in the troubles of the reigns of Richard I. and John, and died at Rouen on 16th November, 1207.

<u>72</u>, 22. *Pope Alexander and Octavian.* Alexander III., elected Pope on 7 September, 1159, was obliged to leave Italy in 1162, on account of the power of the Anti-Pope Octavian, and did not return until the decease of the latter in 1164. Samson's journey to Rome was, therefore, between 1159 and 1162, before he became a professed monk.

<u>73</u>, 3. *Pretended to be Scotch.* Mr. Arnold gives as the reason for this that "the Scottish kingdom at this time naturally sided with Octavian, England being in favour of Alexander" (I. xliii.). It has been suggested that "simulavi me esse Scottum" in the text means that Samson pretended to be an *Irishman*, the name Scotus having originally signified Irish, only acquiring its present meaning with the immigration of the Scots from the North of Ireland into Argyll, and their growth into a powerful nation. Bromton, speaking of Ireland, says:—"Dicta est eciam aliquando Scotia a Scotis eam inhabitantibus, priusquam ad aliam Scotiam Britannicam devenerunt; unde in Martirologio legitur: Tali die apud Scotiam natalis Sanctæ Brigidæ: quod est, apud Hiberniam" (see Twysden, *Historiæ Anglicanæ Scriptores X*, London 1652: vol. I., col. 1072, l. 11). When therefore this passage was written (the fourteenth century) it is clear that the usage of Scot as meaning Irishman was not understood, and was regarded as needing explanation. Samson's contemporary, Ralph de Diceto, following the account of Henry of Huntingdon, twice explains that the Scots came from Ireland (ed. Stubbs 1876, I. 10; II. 34). This explanation again implies that by the middle and end of the twelfth century the word had come to mean exclusively "Scotsman." The same opinion is expressed by Burton: "It is not safe to count that the word Scot must mean a native of present Scotland, when the period dealt with is earlier than the middle of the twelfth century" (*History of Scotland*, 1873, I. 207). In that part of the Anglo-Saxon Chronicle which was compiled during the reign of King Alfred, Scot regularly means Irishman. In A.D. 903 the death is noted of Virgil, abbot of the Scots, i.e. Irish: but this appears to

be the last instance of the use of the word in the Chronicle in that sense. Between the years 924 and 1138 the word Scot occurs fourteen and Scotland twenty-six times in the Chronicle, always with the modern significance.

73, 6. *Gaveloc.* Javelin, a word of Celtic origin, but not specifically Scotch. Matthew Paris speaks of it in 1256 as a Frisian weapon: "Frisiones cum jaculis quæ vulgariter gavelocos appellant." (Chr. Maj. ed. Luard. v. 550.) In the Romance of Percival by Chrestien de Troyes, is the couplet, "Et il, qui bien lancier savoit, De gaverlos que il avoit." (Ed. Potvin, Tome I. lines 1309-10. Mons, 1866).

73, 10. *Ride, Ride Rome, turn Cantwereberi,* This is written in English by Jocelin; and its meaning seems to be "I am riding towards Rome, turning from Canterbury." Arnold (I. xliii.) says, "If he had meant to say 'returning to Canterbury,' he would at once have been taken for an English adherent of Alexander."

74, 12. *Geoffrey Ridel.* This presentation appears to have been made (c. 1161) by Henry II., perhaps during Samson's journey abroad. In 1163 Geoffrey became Archdeacon of Canterbury in succession to Thomas à Becket, appointed Archbishop, and for the next eight years was in violent opposition to his primate, who called him "our arch-devil," and excommunicated him. On May 1, 1173, Geoffrey was chosen Bishop of Ely, and died at Winchester, 27 July, 1189. As Geoffrey from the chronicles seems to have been of a masterful and contumacious spirit, it must have given Abbot Samson peculiar satisfaction to have got the better of him over the timber referred to on page 106.

74, 19. *Acre.* This was Samson's first imprisonment at Castleacre (circ. 1161, before he became a monk). His second imprisonment probably took place about 1173, as on page 6 he speaks of it to Jocelin, then a novice, as something quite recent. As to Castleacre, see note on pages 223-4.

CHAPTER VII.

77, 23. *Charters of the King.* This dispute with the monks of Canterbury, heard before King Henry II. on the 11th February, 1187, raised the whole question of the Liberty of St. Edmund, a matter respecting which the Bury monastery was extremely tenacious. A marginal note in the original MS. of the Chronicle, against the puzzled phrase of the King (see page 78, lines 1-3), says: "Our Charter speaks of the time of King Edward, and of the time of his mother, Queen Emma, who had eight and a half hundreds as a marriage portion before the time of King Edward, besides Mildenhall." According to the *Anglo-Saxon Chronicle*, the Confessor, after his coronation in 1043, seized the possessions of his mother, "because she was formerly very hard on the King her son, and did less for him than he wished before he was King, and also since." The Franchise having thus come into the Confessor's hands, was granted to the Abbots and Monks of Bury shortly after his accession. Under a Charter of King Edmund granted about 945, and Charters of Canute and Hardicanute, the jurisdiction of Bury Abbey had been restricted to the town, and the circuit indicated by the four crosses placed at the distance of a mile from the extremities of the town: but by the Confessor's Charter, it was enlarged to a district extending over about two-fifths of the whole county of Suffolk. (For names of the 8½ hundreds included in the Liberty see note on page 232, 14.)

Edward the Confessor paid a visit to the shrine of St. Edmund in 1044, and when he had come within a mile of it, dismounted from his horse and accomplished the rest of the journey on foot. Herman the archdeacon, who wrote about half a century later, is the first to relate this fact, and also the grant by the King to the abbey of the 8½ hundreds: "Qua tunc suffragatorem reditibus imperialibus honorat, centurias quas Anglice hundrez vocant, octo et semis sibi circum-circa se donat, regiamque mansionem nomine Mildenhall his adauget" (Arnold, I. 48). The original grant of Edward the Confessor gave the abbey jura regalia in wide loose general terms. Later, Charters became gradually more explicit as to the extent of jurisdiction (civil and criminal) conferred. Later still, the Royal justices in eyre supervened. The institution of the circuits and assizes had to be fitted into the exempt jurisdiction: so the Liberty had its own assizes, etc., but outside the interior special and inviolable circuit of the bannaleuca or limits of St. Edmundsbury itself.

Lord Francis Hervey, who has made a special study of the subject, gives hope on page 250 of his notes to the *Breviary of Suffolk* (1902), of his undertaking "a detailed examination of the history and incidents of the great Liberty of St. Edmund, which remained in the hands of its monastic rulers till the day when Abbot Reeve surrendered his Abbey to Henry VIII., November 4, 1539."

78, 15. Matthew xix. 12.

78, 16. *the matter was put off.* This dispute between Bury and Canterbury was not, as a matter of fact, ultimately composed till over 200 years later. Amongst Dr. Yates' manuscript materials for the never completed Part II. of his *History of Bury* is a memorandum (now amongst the Egerton MSS. in the British Museum) in the following words:—

"The Letters Patent of King Henry 4th the 25th Nov. 1408 confirm and ratify an Indenture of three parts between the Archbishop of Canterbury, the Prior of Christ Church, Canterbury, and the Abbot of Bury St. Edmund's, by which it is determined that the parishes of Hadleygh et Illeygh being within the eight hundreds and an half called the Liberty or Franchise of St. Edmund should be subject to the Abbot's Seneschallus, or High Steward of the Franchise, and that the return of the writs of the Seneschal's Great Court with the rolls fines and other rights and privileges should be regarded in those parishes in the same manner as in the other parts of the Liberty. An exemption on the part of the Archbishop having been claimed, this indenture terminated a dispute that had been above 160 years [cf. Arnold, III. 188] in agitation. During this dispute it was agreed that the Sheriff of Suffolk should act till its termination as Seneschal of these Parishes. A patent was addressed to the Sheriff of Suffolk dated 27th November in the same year, commanding him no longer to intromit within the Franchise of St. Edmund, but to preserve inviolate the Liberties and immunities of the Abbot and Monastery.—*Registrum Rubrum in Collect, Burien.*: 317 *to* 328 *inclusive.*"

78, 16. Et adhuc sub judice lis est. Horace, *Arte Poet.*, 78.

79, 6. *Bishop of Ely.* This was William of Longchamp (d. 1197), once described by Henry II. as a "son of two traitors." He fled the kingdom in 1191 on his fall from power, came to England in 1192, but was not permitted to proceed further than Canterbury, and crossed the seas again. In 1193 he returned, bearing letters from the Emperor, and met the Regency at St. Albans. It was on this occasion that he passed through St. Edmundsbury, as recorded on page 80. In Normandy, at the instigation of the Archbishop of Rouen, he had been everywhere received as an excommunicated person (cf. Rokewode, page 127).

79, 10. *Archbishopric vacant.* Archbishop Baldwin died at Acre, in November, 1190; his successor Reginald, Bishop of Bath, was elected in December, 1191, and died after a few days. Hubert Walter, with whom Samson afterwards came into conflict, was elected Archbishop in May, 1192 (see note on page 245).

80, 12. *Archbishop of York.* This was Geoffrey, the half-brother of Richard I., to whom he had sworn that he would not return to England without the King's leave. Having returned, he was, on his landing at Dover in September, 1191, arrested by Longchamp's orders, and thrown into prison.

80, 24. *King Henry had taken the Cross.* At the interview of Henry II. with Philip of France, between Trie and Gisors, the two Kings took the cross upon the Feast of St Agnes, 21 January, 1188.

82, 8. *War throughout England.* After John's return from France in 1193, the country was in a state of general warfare; and Windsor was besieged by the Regency with the King's other castles.

82, 16. *His own standard.* See note to p. 85, l. 25, below.

<u>83</u>, 1. *Licence for holding tournaments.* This was little more than a device for raising money. In 1194 Richard ordered tournaments to be held, in order to practise the knights in warfare. No one could joust at a tournament without a licence; and the price of the licence varied with the rank of the holder.

<u>85</u>, 12. *Withgar.* This great thane, who is styled in the Cartulary of Abbot John of Northwold "the famous Earl," had the custody for Queen Emma, mother of Edward the Confessor, of the franchise of the eight hundreds and a half which subsequently constituted the Liberty of St. Edmund (see notes on pages 232 and 238). Mr. Rokewode says (p. 129): "The honour of Clare was composed chiefly of the great possessions in Suffolk and Essex of Alfric, son of Withgar or Wisgar (*Liber Domesday*)."

<u>85</u>, 25. *Standard of St. Edmund.* In the famous Harleian MS. 2278, the original book containing the metrical life of St. Edmund by John Lydgate, presented to Henry VI. by Bury Abbey after his visit to the monastery in 1433, there is a pictorial representation of this Standard. It depicts Adam and Eve on either side of the Tree of Knowledge, and the devil with a human face and a serpent's body curled round the tree. Above the tree is a lamb and a cross, with crescents in the background. The counterseal of Abbot Samson also has the lamb and cross (see page 229).

<u>86</u>, 6. *Earl Roger Bigot.* This Earl was son of Hugh, the rebellious baron. It appears from the text that the Standard of St. Edmund was carried by him into the fight at the battle of Fornham, in October, 1173 (see p. 1).

<u>86</u>, 18. *Robert of Cockfield.* References to members of this family of Cockfield, or Cokefield, appear often in the *Chronicle.* The dispute as to rights which arose on Robert's death is told again in greater detail at the end of the *Chronicle,* by William of Diss (see pp. 254-6), and the dispute as to the wardship of the daughter of Adam, son of Robert, on pages 187-8. Nothing here arises except Samson's denial of Adam's right of hereditary tenure, in which he was successful.

<u>87</u>, 16. *Eight and a half hundreds.* See notes to p. 44, l. 14, and p. 77, l. 23, on the Liberty of St. Edmund (pp. 232, 238).

<u>88</u>, 16. *Haberdon.* This is a field (still called by the same name) in the south-east corner of the town, with remains of earthworks. It was held in monastic times of the sacrist by the singular tenure, that the tenant should find a white bull as often as a gentlewoman should visit the shrine of St. Edmund "to make the oblation of the said white bull," with a view to secure a favourable answer to her prayers for offspring. On these occasions the bull was led from his pasture on the Haberdon through the principal streets of the town in procession to the Church of St. Edmund.

CHAPTER VIII.

<u>101</u>-105. The whole of this Chapter is obviously an interpolation in the Chronicle by some monk other than Jocelin himself. The story of Henry of Essex is included in the long and elaborate "vita et passio cum miraculis Sancti Edmundi" prepared in the fourteenth century in the monastery at Bury, and now preserved in the Bodleian Library (MS. 240); and at the end of this transcript the compiler adds, "Cuius narracionem Jocelinus audiens, in scriptis redegit" (*Nova Legenda Anglie*, ed. Horstman, 1901, II. 637). It is apparent from the opening phrase of the text (p. 105) that Jocelin, who most probably went to Reading in the train of the Abbot, commenced to set down the story at the bidding of Samson, but left its completion to some other monk of inferior degree. Perhaps this was William of Diss, who added at the end of the Chronicle (see pages 254-6) a declaration as to the lands of Robert of Cockfield.

<u>101</u>, 10. *precept of Seneca.* Mr. Arnold says: "Many things resembling this sentiment occur in the 109th Epistle of Seneca; but probably the passage is somewhere else in his works."

<u>103</u>, 18. *thrown down the standard.* Henry of Essex's act of cowardice took place in 1157, during an expedition into Flintshire, when the Welsh made a sudden attack. His dropping the standard brought King Henry II. and the Royal army into great peril (Gervase, i. 165, Rolls ed.).

<u>104</u>, 1. *Roger Earl of Clare.* There seems to be an attempt at punning, at this point, by the monk who wrote the original story in Latin: "Rogerus comes Clarensis, clarus genere et militari clarior exercitis, cum suis Clarensibus maturius occurrisset."

<u>104</u>, 9. *trial of battle.* This fight between Henry of Essex and Robert de Montfort took place in 1163 (Ralph de Diceto, *Ymag. Hist.* i. 310, Rolls ed.), on an eyot in the Thames, and is still traditionally remembered at Reading.

CHAPTER IX

<u>106</u>, 6. *stay at Melford.* The manor of Melford was given to the monastery in the time of Leofstan (second Abbot) by Earl Alfric, the son of Withgar (Parker's *History of Long Melford*, p. 1). At Long Melford, 13 miles south of Bury, was a country house belonging to the Abbots of Bury; and at the present Melford Hall there are said to be still some relics of this occupancy. After Samson died, in 1211, there was a dispute that lasted a considerable time as to the validity of the election of Hugo, his successor; and the Papal Legate, Nicholas, Bishop of Tusculum, who tried vainly to compose it, stayed for some time at Melford (Arnold, ii. 46). Abbot Simon of Luton died at his manor of Melford in April, 1279.

<u>108</u>, 8, 13. *forty pounds a year from the town.* Battely prints (*App.* xvii. 149) a letter from Pope Eugenius III. (no date) addressed to Helyas, the sacrist

(Ording's nephew), confirming Ording's instructions as to the rents of the town being applied to the service of the Altar.

112, 8. *Charter from King Henry the Second.* "All the men of London shall be quit and free, and all their goods throughout England, and the ports of the sea, of and from all toll and passage and lestage and all other customs" (Charter Henry I.). "All the citizens of London shall be quit from toll and lastage throughout all England and the ports of the sea" (Charter of Henry II.—confirmed by Charter of Richard I., 23 April, 1194, and by Charter of John, 17 June, 1199). (Birch's *Historical Charters of the City of London*, 1887, pp. 3, 5.)

112, 15. *theam* (Lat. themus, team). The right of compelling a person in whose hands stolen property was found to say from whom he received it (Glossary in Stubbs's *Select Charters*).

113, 10. Judges xvi. 9.

116, 15. *A charter was made.* The text of this Charter of 1194, granted by Samson to the Burgesses, will be found in Battely (*App.* xxii. 155-6) and in the *Monasticon*, iii. 153. It confirms to the town all the customs and liberties which it had in the times of Henry II. and his predecessors; and it declares that with regard to watch and ward and the custody of the gates, the ancient custom is that the town shall furnish eight watchmen night by night, all the year round, two for each ward, and a larger number at Christmas and on St. Edmund's Day [20 November]; also that the town should find four gatekeepers for the four gates, the fifth or eastern gate being in the custody of the Abbot. Nothing is said in the Charter about the appointment of the portreeves; but the right of burgesses to sue and be sued in their own borough-court (portmanne-mot), instead of going outside the borough to the hundred-mot or the shire-mot, is insisted upon. "What is evidently assumed is that the portreeve is the Abbot's servant, and administers justice in the Abbot's name" (Arnold, II. xxxix.).

CHAPTER X

119, 10. Lamentations iv. i.

121, 12. *Abbot Robert.* This was Robert II. (fourth Abbot), a monk of Westminster, elected by the convent in 1102, but not confirmed by Henry I. until 1107. He died shortly afterwards, on the 16th September, 1107, and, after an interregnum of seven years, Albold, Prior of St. Nicasius, at Meaux, succeeded him in the abbacy. Robert was buried in the Infirmary Chapel (Douai MS.). For his character and labours, see MS. quoted in Arnold, i. 356.

121, 20. *Hubert Walter.* Hubert's father, Harvey Walter, was descended from Hubert, the first Norman settler, who received at the Conquest grants of land in Norfolk and Suffolk. Hubert is said to have been born at West Dereham, in Norfolk (Tanner, *Not. Monast. Norfolk*, xxi.), where lived, as will be seen from the text (p. 121, l. 25), his mother Matilda de Valognes (whose sister Bertha married Ranulf de Glanville). He was brought up in Glanville's household, and was so much in his confidence that he was afterwards said to have "shared with him in the government of England." In 1186 he became Dean of York, and in 1189 Bishop of Salisbury. In 1190 he went to the Holy Land, returning in 1193, in which year he was elected Archbishop of Canterbury and appointed justiciary. Richard's departure over sea in 1194 left him virtual ruler of England for the next few years. He died in 1205; and in March, 1890, a tomb opened in Canterbury Cathedral was found to contain his remains.

124, 6. *The Pope wrote.* This letter of Innocent III. was dated 1st December, 1198, and was addressed (not to the Archbishop but) to the Abbot and convent of St. Edmund (*Migne's Patrologia*, vol. ccxiv., No. 457 of the Regesta).

CHAPTER XI

134, 13. Tendens ad sidera palmas. Virgil, *Æn.* i. 93.

135, 18. *Anniversary obit of the Abbot Robert.* According to the *Liber Albus*, fol. 35, the anniversary of Abbot Robert was "xvi Kal. Octobris" (16th September). The anniversaries of Ording and Hugh, mentioned in line 20, were 31st January and the 16th November.

139, 20. *Chapel of St. Denis.* This chapel was at the west end of the church, probably north of the great western tower, with a chapel dedicated to St. Faith above it. Abbot Baldwin, who commenced the erection of the basilica, was a monk of St. Denis; hence, no doubt, the dedication of a chapel to that saint.

CHAPTER XII

142, 5. *Church of Coventry.* Hugh de Nonant (d. 1198), Bishop of Lichfield and Coventry, had a violent dislike to all monks, and, whenever he could, put secular canons in their place. He had turned out the monks at Coventry, and Pope Celestine III. appointed in 1197 a Commission, on which Samson sat, for restoring these expelled monks. The monks were re-inducted by Archbishop Hubert Walter on 18th January, 1198.

144, 1. *Church of Wetherden.* This deed is recorded in the Feet of Fines for Suffolk, 9 Richard I., No. 49.

144, 9. *master of the schools.* A perpetual pension of three marcs, payable from the tithes of Wetherden to "the master of the school at St. Edmund," was granted in 1198 by John, Bishop of Norwich, at the request of Samson (*Curtey's Register*, Brit. Mus. fol. 119).

145, 24. *Chapel of St. Andrew.* According to the *Gesta Sacristarum* (Arnold, ii. 291) the Chapel of St. Andrew was for the most part built and finished by the sacrist Hugo under Samson, and seems to have been then connected with the infirmary (iii. 87). Later on it was removed into the cemetery of the monks (iii. 187).

145, 25. *Chapels of St. Katherine and St. Faith.* Two chapels at the west end; St. Katherine to the south, over the chapel of St. John, St. Faith to the north, over the chapel of St. Denis.

147, 19. Tractant fabrilia fabri. Horace, *Ep.* ii. i. 116.

147, 20. *Adam of Cockfield.* This was the claimant whose case is reported on pp. 86-8, and again (by William of Diss) on pp. 254-6. An elaborate pedigree of the Cockfield family is given by Rokewode on pp. 140-8 of his book. His daughter's name was Nesta, and, as stated at p. 187, l. 24, she became, on her father's death in 1198, the ward and wife of Thomas de Burgh, brother of Hubert the chamberlain, who was afterwards justiciary and Earl of Kent. Nesta married three times, and died about 1248.

149, 3. Munera (crede mihi) capiunt hominesque deosque; Placatur donis Jupiter ipse datis. Ovid, *Arte Amandi*, iii. 653.

CHAPTER XIII

151, 13. *Portman-moot.* Borough court. Written in English in the original Chronicle ("portmane-mot.")

151, 18. *Sorpeni.* Payment for grass for a cow.

152, 5. *Ording who lies there.* Ording (d. 1156) was one of six abbots who were buried in the Chapter House, and whose names are recorded in the MS., circa 1425, discovered by Dr. Montagu James at Douai (*James*, p. 180). The original chapter house of the monastery was built by Godefridus, the sacrist, about 1107. There was a fire which destroyed all the convent buildings, and Helyas, the sacrist, Ording's nephew, "reformavit ad plenum" the chapter house. His uncle was the first Abbot buried there. Ording's place of sepulture was nearest to the east end or dais. Hugo and Samson, Ording's successors, were also buried in Helyas's chapter house: Samson being, according to the Douai MS. "sepultus in capitulo sedes ad pedes Ric. Abb. sub lapidibus marmoreis ut suprascriptum est de Abb. Ordingo." About 1220 Richard of Newport, then sacrist, "vetus capitulum destruxit, et novum a fundamentis construxit." (Arnold, II. 293.) Afterwards Richard of Insula (1229-34), Henry of Rushbrook (1234-46), and Edmund of Walpole (1248-56) were also buried in the chapter house. Its dimensions, according to William of Worcester's measurements in 1479, were 60 paces by 20. In the course of some recent excavations (1902-3) the coffins of five of the above Abbots, and much worked stone and marble, have been found on the site of this chapter house.

152, 19. *tenant of the cellarer, by name Ketel.* As Ketel dwelt "without the gate," he was, being "of the cellarer's fee," subject to the "judicial duel" which William I. had introduced; whereas the argument of his fellow-burgesses seems to have been that if he had dwelt within the borough he would have been tried and acquitted or condemned by the "oaths of his neighbours"— the compurgators out of whom our jury system grew. The monks recognized that the time had come when the franchise of the town should be extended to the rural possessions of the Abbey, and all brought under a common jurisdiction.

153, 6. *within the jurisdiction.* "Infra bannamleucam," defined by Ducange as a certain territory by the boundaries of which the jurisdiction and immunities of any place, whether a town or monastery, were limited. *Bannum* is here used in the sense of jurisdiction; and the amount of territory so enfranchised was usually reckoned as a league either way, hence banna leuca or banlieue. The exempt jurisdiction of Bury Abbey was limited to the circuit of a mile within four crosses.

153, 6. *Villeins of Hardwick.* The Latin word is *lancettos,* serfs holding by base services. In one of the cartularies of St. Edmund, the "Lancetti de Hardwick" were to cleanse the latrines of the monastery.

154, 23. *Beodricsworth.* This is the ancient name of Bury St. Edmunds. Mr. Arnold says (I. iv.) the name of Beodric "seems to mean 'a table chieftain,' *comp.* beod. geneat, a table companion. But there is some countenance in the MSS. for Beadricsworth, which would come from beadu-rica, one mighty in war." Seynt Edmunds Biri is first substituted for Beodricsworth in Charters from Edward the Confessor to the Monastery (cf. page 260 and Battely, *App.* ix. 134).

155, 14. *Aver-peni.* The money paid by the tenant in commutation of the service (avera) of performing any work for his lord by horse or ox, or by carriage with either.

155, 20. *Eels from Southrey.* Ælgiva, Queen of Canute, gave to the Monastery yearly four thousand eels, with her gifts which pertained thereto at Lakenheath. The manor of Southrey, in Norfolk, with three fisheries, was appropriated to the cellarer (Rokewode, p. 151).

157, 2. *haggovele.* Probably head-tax or hearth-tax.

159, 2. Romans xii. 10.

159, 9. Summa petit livor. Ovid, *Rem. Amoris,* 369.

CHAPTER XIV

<u>163</u>, 8. Habakkuk iii. 2.

<u>164</u>, 11. *Chest with the shirt of St. Edmund.* Archdeacon Herman, in his treatise *De Miraculis Sancto Eadmundi* (Arnold, i. 26 *et seq.*), describes how Leofstan (2nd Abbot) decided to open the coffin containing St. Edmund's body and examine the remains. The body was found covered with a vestment stained with blood and pierced with arrows. This was taken off and the body wrapped in a linen sheet. In the continuation of Herman's work, ascribed to Samson himself, there is an account of another Herman, a monk of Bury, and a popular preacher, who displayed irreverently certain relics of St. Edmund. He took the shirt out of its casket, and unfolded it for the people to kiss. Tolinus the sacrist commented severely on the occurrence, and on the third day at sunset Herman died. The "feretrum cum camisia S. Edmundi" was amongst the relics carried in procession round the Church on Christmas Day, Palm Sunday, Easter Day, and probably other high festivals (Rituale, Harl. MS. 297, cent, xiv., quoted by *James*, p. 183).

<u>165</u>, 1. *Cup of St. Edmund.* To drinking from this cup various miracles are ascribed: a rich lady cured after long suffering from fever; a Dunwich man with dropsy; a girl afflicted with a great swelling, who drinks from the cup thrice in the name of the Trinity; a Cluniac monk of St. Saviour's, Southwark, named Gervasius, whose story is told in great detail in Samson's *De Miraculis* (Arnold, i. 202-3). It is said that an indulgence *toties quoties* was granted to pilgrims who drank from this cup "in the worshippe of God and Saint Edmund," hence its name of "Pardon Bowl"; but I have not found the original authority for this.

<u>165</u>, 19. Luke xii. 2.

<u>166</u>, 9. Psalm lxiii. 11.

<u>170</u>, 4. Isaiah i. 2.

<u>171</u>, 18. *verse inscribed.* In the *Cronica Burienis* (Arnold, iii. 8) this verse is given in a slightly different form—"Martyris ecce zoma Michaelis servet agalma," the writer adding, "Agalma, id est, sacra receptacula divinitatis." "Zoma" is probably the Greek word "soma," body. But it has also been translated "garment," and Carlyle's version of the inscription (*Past and Present*, ch. xvi.) is, "This is the Martyr's garment, which Michael's Image guards." Lord Francis Hervey, in his edition (1902) of Recce's *Breviary of Suffolk*, says, "Having regard to the fondness of the mediæval versifiers for rhyme, I feel tempted to suggest that the word may have been 'salma,' a word of unknown origin, which in Italian means corpse.... The verse in question was most probably not home made, and was not clearly intelligible to the monks themselves."

<u>171</u>, 21. *iron rings.* This phrase is somewhat obscure: "annuli ferrei sicut solebat fieri in cista Norensi." Ducange gives "Norrensis" as an occasional equivalent for Northmannus, hence Mr. Arnold suggests for cista Norensis "a Norwegian chest" (i. 311).

<u>175</u>, 10. *Ailwin the monk.* Ailwin, also written Egelwin, was keeper of the shrine of St. Edmund before the foundation of the Abbey. In view of the invasion of England by the Danish chief Turchil, Ailwin fled, in 1010, from Beodricsworth to London with the body of St. Edmund, returning 1014. In 1050 Ailwin, then a very aged man, was invited by Abbot Leofstan to come from Hulme to Bury to identify the body of the Saint.

<u>176</u>, 18. *Keeper of St. Botolph.* There was a chapel (probably on the south side of the presbytery) dedicated to St. Botolph, in which was the shrine with the relics of that Saint.

<u>177</u>, 3. Felix, quem faciunt aliena pericula cautum. Erasmus, *Adagia.*

CHAPTER XV

<u>178</u>, 6. *King John ... came down to St. Edmund.* John paid several visits to Bury Abbey during Samson's abbacy: once in 1199, immediately after his coronation, when he made the miserable offering described by Jocelin on p. 178; a second time in 1201, when returning from Northumberland; a third time in 1203, when, according to Rokewode (p. 154), "he made a pilgrimage to St. Edmund's, at the feast of St. Thomas the Apostle, and gave the convent ten marcs annually, payable from the exchequer, for the repairs of the shrine of St. Edmund, in consideration of the monks giving back to the King, for his life, a sapphire and ruby, which he had offered to the Saint, and which were to revert to the convent." In connection with the disputed question of the nomination of Samson's successor (which lasted for over two years), John came to Bury on November 4, 1114, and meeting the monks in the chapter house, made them a speech as to his own rights in the matter, which is recorded in Arnold, II. xv. and 95-6.

<u>180</u>, 7. Isaiah i. 2.

<u>182</u>, 3. Matthew xii. 25.

<u>183</u>, 9. In te vindicassem nisi iratus fuissem. Cic. *Tusc.* iv. 36.

<u>183</u>, 14. Mark iv. 39.

<u>187</u>, 20. *seisin of the damsel.* There was another claimant for the wardship of Nesta of Cockfield, not here mentioned, viz., King Richard I., who (see pp. 148-9) was defied by Samson, but was appeased by a present of some horses, dogs, and other valuable gifts. "Here you may see what misery followeth the

tenure by Knight's service: if the tenant dieth, leaving his heir within age, how the poor child may be tossed and tumbled, chopped and changed, bought and sold like a jade in Smithfield, and what is more, married to whom it pleaseth his guardian, whereof ensue many evils" (Rastell: *Terms of the Lawes of this Realm*, ed. 1579, fol. 98).

189, 6. Decipi quadam specie recti. Horace, *De Arte Poetica*, 25.

189, 8. Isaiah xlii. 8.

189, 9. *Abbot of Cluny*. This was Hugh, Abbot of Reading from 1180 to 1199, when he was appointed Abbot of Cluny. Much information about him may be found in Dr. J. B. Hurry's admirable *History of Reading Abbey*, 1901, whence the following note as to precedence is taken: "Sir Henry Englefield (*Archaeologia*, vol. vi. p. 61) states that the Abbot of Reading took precedence after the Abbots of Glastonbury and St. Albans. But it is probable that no such definite order was observed.... In the Articles of Faith under Convocation, 28 Henry VIII., the following is the order of signatures—St. Albans, Westminster, St. Edmunds Bury, Glastonbury, Reading."

CHAPTER XVI.

190, 6. Numbers xi. 26.

191, 1. *When the Prior died.* Mr. Rokewode assigns Robert's death to 1200, perhaps because the narrative of the election of his successor follows in the Chronicle the account of the visit to the monastery of Hugh, Abbot of Cluny.

192, 9. Proverbs xix. 11.

193, 19. Deut. xvii. 8.

196, 19. *[Herbert] the new prior.* This election seems to have taken place in 1200. After Samson's death in 1211, Herbert had a great deal of anxiety arising out of King John's refusal to accept the choice of Hugh II. (then Prior of Westminster and afterwards Bishop of Ely) as Abbot; and the narrative of the *Electio Hugonis* takes up 102 pages of Mr. Arnold's vol. ii. Herbert died in September, 1220, and was succeeded as Prior by Richard of Insula (afterwards 12th Abbot).

197, 20. Acts xxvi. 24.

197, 23. Nihil omne parte beatum. Hor. *Odes*, i. 16.

198, 7. Exitus acta probabit. Ovid, *Heroides*, ii. 85.

198, 11. Psalm lxiv. 3.

199, 5. Fallitur augurio spes bona sæpe suo. Ovid, *Heroides*, xvii. 234.

CHAPTER XVII.

<u>200</u>, 8. Deut. xvi. 19.

<u>200</u>, 16. Galatians v. 9.

<u>201</u>, 20. *Dean of London.* This quotation from the *Ymagines Historiarum* of Ralph de Diceto, Dean of St. Paul's, who died about 1202, is interesting, as showing that apparently a manuscript copy of that work was in the possession of Bury Abbey shortly after its compilation. Diceto has often been identified with Diss in Norfolk: and there are evidences that William of Diss had a good deal to do with Jocelin's Chronicle (cf. pages 242, 254). Bishop Stubbs thinks that Diceto is "an artificial name, adopted by its bearer as the Latin name of a place with which he was associated," and this he suggests may be one of three places in Maine.

<u>202</u>, 16. Mutans quadrata rotundis. Hor. *Ep.* i. 1, 100.

<u>203</u>, 16. Pila minantia pilis. *Lucan*, 1, 7.

<u>204</u>, 13. *By his writ.* The same difficulty as to jurisdiction that arose in the case of Monk's Eleigh with Christ Church, Canterbury (see chapter vii. and notes to p. 77, l. 23, and p. 78, l. 16) occurred with the Bishop of Ely; and it lasted an equally long time. In the *Excerpta Cantabrigiensia* (Arnold, III. 188) is a long account of a "Contentio inter monasterium S. Edmundi et episcopum Eliensum" (Univ. Lib. Ff. 2, 29) respecting the return to writs affecting places within the Liberty of St. Edmund. The Bishop claimed that when a writ came down to the Sheriff of Suffolk referring to a place which, though within the liberty of St. Edmund, belonged to the see of Ely, it was the duty of the sheriff to send that writ for execution, not to the abbot, but to the bishop; and the abbot claimed that the ancient jurisdiction of St. Edmund would thus be infringed. Since the liberty of St. Edmund comprised eight and a half hundreds in the county of Suffolk, within which hundreds the see of Ely possessed many manors, it is obvious that if the charge and execution of writs affecting these manors were withheld from the abbot and given to the bishop, the jurisdiction of St. Edmund would be to that extent impaired and restricted. The Contentio begins with a reference to the King's decision just given (1408) in favour of Bury against the Canterbury monks (see note on page 239), and goes on to describe the efforts made by Abbot Cratfield to stop the encroachments of Bishop Fordham of Ely, with whom he proposes a meeting, from which the bishop excuses himself. The controversy dragged on, with many adjournments and delays, all of which the (Bury) writer lays to the charge of the other side: nor was it concluded at the date (1426 or 1427) when the tract was written (Arnold, III. xviii.-xix.).

<u>205</u>, 20. Psalm viii. 8.

<u>207</u>, 7. *Geoffrey Fitz-Peter and William de Stutville.* These were important officials, whom John could ill spare. Geoffrey Fitz-Peter, Earl of Essex (died 1213) was justiciar, having been appointed by Richard I. to this high office in 1198, on the resignation of Archbishop Hubert Walter. He was confirmed in his appointment by John, who disliked him, but used him for his own ends. William de Stutville had been appointed sheriff of the county of York in 1201, and died in 1203.

<u>209</u>, 20. *made his will just as if he was now to die.* The Royal summons to Court was dated 1203, as the brief of Innocent III. is printed in Migne's *Patrologia*, vol. 214, and is dated 21 January, 1203. Samson lived nearly nine years afterwards; but as to the facts of his latest years we know practically nothing. As to his death and burial, see Preface, pages xl.-xlii.

<u>211</u>, 9. Pollicitis dives quilibet esse potest. Ovid., *De Arte Amandi*, 1. 444.

<u>211</u>. At the foot of fol. 163 of the *Liber Albus*, from which Jocelin's Chronicle is taken, is a memorandum by William of Diss, which, as it has been printed both by Rokewode and Arnold, is translated below, though it is not by Jocelin. It is merely an expansion of the story told by Jocelin himself on pp. 86-8. Adam of Cockfield wanted to claim his father's lands by hereditary right; but William of Diss gives the evidence against this claim. The succession was: Lenmere, Adam the first (married Adeliza), Robert (died 1191), Adam the claimant (died 1198), who married Rohesia, and had a daughter Nesta, over whose wardship there was the dispute recorded on page 187.

"Robert of Cockfield acknowledged to my lord abbot Samson, in the presence of many persons—Master W. of Banham, brother W. of Diss, chaplains, William of Breiton, and many others—that he had no hereditary right in the vills of Groton and Semere. For in the days of King Stephen, when the peace was disturbed, the monks of St. Edmund, with the consent of the abbot, granted the aforesaid two vills to Adam of Cockfield, his father, to be held all the days of his life: Semere for the annual payment of one hundred shillings, and Groton by the payment of an annual rent, because Adam could defend the aforesaid towns against the holders of the neighbouring castles, W. of Milden and W. of Ambli, in that he had a castle of his own near to the aforesaid manors, namely, the castle of Lelesey.

"After the death of the aforesaid Adam, they granted the said manors to Robert of Cockfield, son of Adam, at a double rate for Semere, that is an annual rent of ten pounds, so long as the lords abbots and the convent wish. But he never had a charter for it, not even to the end of his life. He had good charters for all the tenements which he held of St. Edmund by hereditary right, which charters I, William, known as William of Diss, at that time chaplain, read, in the hearing of many, in the presence of the aforesaid abbot:

that is for the lands of Lelesey, which Ulfric of Lelesey held of St. Edmund in the same township; the charter of the abbot and convent concerning the socages of Rougham, which Mistress Rohesia of Cockfield, once wife of Adam the younger, brought as her dowry; for the lands also which Lenmere, his ancestor, held in the town of Cockfield by hereditary right, and which in the time of King Stephen, with the consent of Anselm, abbot of St. Edmund, were changed into half a knight's fee, although at first they had been socages of St. Edmund.

"He had also charters of the abbot and convent of St. Edmund, for the lands which are in the town of St. Edmund; for the land, that is to say, of Hemfrid Criketot, where the houses of Mistress Adeliza were once situated. They have also a hereditary charter for a great messuage, under a payment of twelve pence, where the hall of Adam the first, of Cockfield, was of old situate, with a wooden tower seven times twenty feet in height. It was confirmed to them as hereditary right by the charter of the abbot and convent, in which charter are specified the length and breadth of that place and messuage, to be held by a payment of two shillings. They also hold a hereditary charter for the lands which Robert of Cockfield, son of Odo of Cockfield, now holds in Barton. But they have no charter for the township of Cockfield, that is, for the portion which pertains to the food of the monks of St. Edmund.

"Then there was one brief of King Henry I., in which he commands Abbot Anselm to allow Adam of Cockfield the first to hold in peace the farm of Cockfield, and others, as long as he pays rents in full; and that brief was sealed only of one part, representing the royal form—against the form of all royal briefs.

"But Robert of Cockfield claimed, in the presence of the lord abbot and the aforesaid, that he believed Cockfield to be his hereditary right on account of his long tenure: because his grandfather, Lenmere, held that manor for a long time before his death, and Adam the first, his son, for the term of his life, and he, Robert, all his life—well-nigh sixty years; but they never had a charter of the abbot or the convent of St. Edmund for the aforesaid land."

APPENDIX III
TABLE OF CHIEF DATES IN THE HISTORY OF THE ABBEY OF ST. EDMUNDSBURY, FROM A.D. 870 TO 1903.

[*Editor's Note.*—I had originally contemplated printing only the dates included in Section II. of this Table, but at the suggestion of the general Editor of the series, I have extended it backwards and forwards so as to give a rapid *aperçu* of the history of Bury Abbey from its earliest beginnings up to the present date. The Table may have a use other than for readers of *Jocelin's Chronicle*, as it brings to a focus a mass of chronological information now scattered over a great variety of books.

For unfortunately there does not exist at present any adequate history of Bury Abbey, one of the most ancient, flourishing and important of the Benedictine institutions in England. There are adequate materials—at any rate for some of the periods of its existence—in the copious manuscripts relating to Bury (many of them formerly belonging to the monastery) now on the shelves of our public libraries and in private hands; and it seems a pity that no one has the courage to undertake a task which, though formidable, has been successfully accomplished in the case of other foundations of less fame.

The names of some of the principal works that may usefully be consulted by students of the history of the Abbey will be found on pp. 276 and 277 at the end of the Table.—E. C.].

SECTION I

BEFORE THE DAYS OF ABBOT SAMSON

870   Nov. 20. Martyrdom of St. Edmund. His head is cut off by the Danes and hidden in a wood "in silvam cui vocabulam est Haglesdun" (*Abbo*, writing 100 years after). [Domesday book (1086) records the existence in Wilford Hundred of a place called Halgestou.] The head being found, is miraculously rejoined to the body, which is buried "in villula Suthtuna [Sutton] dicta, de prope loco martyrizationis" (*Herman*, writing 200 years after).

903	(or later). Relics of St. Edmund removed from the place of burial to Beodricsworth—afterwards called Bury St. Edmunds. The early authorities differ as to this date. Herman says the translation took place in the reign of Athelstan (925-941): the compiler of the Bodl. MS. 240 says A.D. 900 or 906 (*Nov. Leg. Angl.* II. 590); the Curteys Register (Part I. f. 211) says A.D. 903.	
937	(*circa*). According to Abbo, Dunstan, then a youth, hears the story of St. Edmund's death from an old man who said he was the King's standard bearer.	
945	Bishop Theodred (II) of Elmham opens St. Edmund's coffin, finds the body "whole and incorrupt," and places it in a new wooden "loculus" (Abbo).	
945	Charter of King Edmund II (son of Edmund the Elder) granting lands round Beodricsworth to the clerks (*monasterii familia*) who were then guarding St. Edmund's shrine. (Text in Arnold II. 340-1.)	*p.* 238.
985	(*circa*). Dunstan, the Archbishop, tells the story of St. Edmund's martyrdom to others, and Abbo recounts it in his *Passio Sancti Eadmundi*. (Text in Arnold I. 3-25.)	*p.* 217.
1010	Egelwin, or Ailwin, takes the body of the Saint from Beodricsworth to London.	*p.* 175.
1013	Return of Egelwin, with body of St. Edmund, to Beodricsworth.	
1014	February. Death of King Sweyn (according to the chroniclers, at the hands of St. Edmund).	
1020	At the instance of Aelfwin, Bishop of Elmham, the clerks in charge of St. Edmund's shrine are removed, and twenty monks, headed by Uvius, prior of Hulme, installed at Beodricsworth.	

1020	Uvius consecrated 1st abbot of Bury by the Bishop of London.
1020	New stone church (to replace the wooden one containing St. Edmund's body) commenced by order of Canute, in expiation of the sacrilegious behaviour of his father Sweyn towards the saint.
1028	Charter of Canute granting "fundus" or farm at Beodricsworth to be for ever in possession of monks, who were to be free from episcopal jurisdiction. (Text in Arnold II. 340-1).
1032	Oct. 18. Consecration of the new stone church by Egelnoth, Archbishop of Canterbury.
1035	Charter granted to the Abbey by Hardicanute, imposing a fine of "thirty talents of gold" on any one found guilty of infringing the Abbey's franchises. (For privileges granted, see Bodl. MS. 240, printed in *Nova Legenda Anglie* II. 607.)
1038	Oct. Body of the Saint removed to King Canute's new church.
1044	Visit of Edward the Confessor to Bury. *p.* 236.
1044	The Confessor grants to Bury abbey jurisdiction over 8½ hundreds in Suffolk, and the manor of Mildenhall, with freedom to choose their abbot. *p.* 238.
1044	Death of Uvius (remains in Infirmary Chapel). Leofstan appointed 2nd abbot.
1065	Death of Leofstan (remains placed in shrine at foot of St. Edmund). Baldwin of St. Denis (physician to Edward the Confessor) appointed 3rd abbot.
1065	Mint established at Bury under grant of Edward the Confessor, in which Beodricsworth is called (apparently for the first time) St. Edmundsbury. "Ic kithe ihu that Ic habbe unnen *p.* 248.

Baldewine Abbot one munetere with innen Seynt Edmunds Biri" (Battely, p. 134).

1071   Abbot Baldwin at Rome: receives from Pope Alexander II a precious altar of porphyry, with special privileges.

1071   Oct. 27. Bull of Pope Alexander II, taking the monks of St. Edmund under the special protection of the Holy See, and forbidding that a bishop's see should ever be established at Beodricsworth. (Text in Arnold I. 344.)

1081   May 31. Charter of William the Conqueror deciding against the claim of Arfast, Bishop of Thetford, to transfer his see to Bury, and granting exemption from episcopal jurisdiction. (Text in Arnold I. 347.)

1086   Domesday Book returns show that the annual value of the Town "ubi quiescit humatus S. Eadmundus rex et martyr gloriosus" was double that of its value under Edward the Confessor, and a larger number of persons were maintained.

1095   Apr. 29. Translation of St. Edmund's body to new and magnificent basilica built by Baldwin and his sacrists Thurstan and Tolinus.

1097   Death of Baldwin: buried in the Abbey church, east of the choir altar.

1098   (*circa*). Herman the Archdeacon compiles his book, *De Miraculis Sancti Eadmundi.*   *p.*
218.

1100   Henry I gives abbacy to Robert, son of Hugh Lupus, Earl of Chester. Robert (I) deposed 1102.

1101   Attempts of Herbert de Losinga, Bishop of Norwich, to fix his see at Bury; finally disposed of 1102.

1102   Robert II, a monk of Westminster, elected 5th abbot. Scheme for Abbey church enlarged.   *p.*
247.

Godefridus the sacrist a man "of almost gigantic stature, great in body but greater still in mind."

1107   Aug. 15. Robert II consecrated by St. Anselm. Dies soon after, 16 Sept.; buried in Infirmary Chapel.

1114   After seven years' interregnum, Albold, prior of St. Nicasius at Meaux, elected 6th abbot: died 1119; buried in Infirmary Chapel.

1120   Charter of Henry I confirming the Charters of Canute and Edward the Confessor.

1121   Anselm, nephew of St. Anselm, elected 7th abbot. In his days the Norman tower of the Abbey was built.

1132   Henry I pays a pilgrimage to the shrine of St. Edmund.

1135   (circa). St. James' Church built by Abbot Anselm, instead of making a pilgrimage to St. James of Compostella. Church consecrated by William Corbeil, Archbishop of Canterbury.

SECTION II

DURING ABBOT SAMSON'S LIFETIME (1135-1211)

1135   SAMSON born at Tottington, near Thetford.

1144   Samson taken by his mother on a pilgrimage to St. Edmund.   p. 56.

1146   Death of Anselm: buried in Infirmary Chapel.

1146   Ording, Prior of St. Edmund, appointed 8th abbot.

1150   Fire, which destroys the conventual buildings—Abbot's palace, refectory, dormitory, the old infirmary, and the chapter-   p. 247.

house. Rebuilt by Helyas the sacrist, Ording's nephew.

1150	(circa). Galfridus de Fontibus writes the tract *De Infantia Sancti Eadmundi*, dedicated to Ording.	*p.* 218.
1153	Eustace, eldest son of King Stephen, plunders some of the lands of the monastery. Dies at Bury.	
1156	Jan. 31. Death of Ording: buried in chapter-house.	*p.* 247.
1156	Hugh, Prior of Westminster, elected 9th abbot. Receives benediction at Colchester from Archbishop of Canterbury.	
1157	Battle of Coleshill: Cowardice of Henry of Essex.	*pp.* 103, 243.
1160	(*circa*). Samson returns from Paris, and made *magister scholarum* or schoolmaster.	*p.* 66.
1160	(*circa*). Samson's visit to Rome.	*pp.* 72, 236.
1161	Jan. 12. Bull of Alexander II, confirming the Abbot and monks of Bury in all their rights and privileges, authorizing appropriation of certain manors to special purposes, etc. Future abbots to be freely elected. In important matters there is to be an appeal to the Holy See. (Text in Arnold III. 78-80.)	
1161	May 22. Brief obtained from Pope Alexander III, confirming the right of the Abbey to the revenues of Woolpit.	*p.* 74.
1163	Abbot Hugh at the Council of Tours, where he usurps the seat of the Abbot of St. Albans.	

2

5

1203	Jan. 31. Samson appointed by the Pope on a commission concerning the dispensation of Crusaders from their vows: and summoned over sea to advise the King on this question.	*pp.* 207- 11.
1203	Dec. 21. John at Bury, and makes valuable offerings: but prevails on convent to grant him for life the use of the jewels which his mother Queen Eleanor had presented to St. Edmund.	*p.* 251.
1208	Mar. 24. Interdict comes into force throughout England.	
1210	Sept. 23. Fall of central tower of Abbey Church.	
1211	Dec. 30. Death of Samson: buried in unconsecrated ground.	*p.* xl.
1213	July. King John expresses a wish for the vacancy to be filled: Hugh (II) of Northwold chosen.	
1214	July 2. Interdict solemnly dissolved.	
1214	Aug. 12. Samson's body exhumed and buried in the chapter-house of Bury Abbey.	*pp.* xlii., 247.

SECTION III

FROM 1214 TO DISSOLUTION IN 1539

| 1214 | Nov. 4. King John at Bury: makes a speech in the chapter-house asserting his rights over the election of abbot. | *p.* 251. |
| 1214 | Nov. 20. The discontented earls and barons meet at Bury (probably on St. Edmund's Day) "as if for prayer." Archbishop Langton reads to them Henry I's charter: and each swears on the high altar to make war on John unless he gives them the liberties contained therein (*Roger of Wendover*, vol. iii. 293-4). | |

1215	Mar. 10. Commissioners appointed by the Pope finally give judgment in favour of Hugh's election as abbot.
1215	June 9. King's approval to appointment of Hugh given in Staines meadow.
1215	June 15. Magna Charta signed.
1215-6	Louis, son of Philip II of France, invited by the barons to help them in their struggle against John. East Anglian towns sacked—Norwich and Lynn by the French; Cambridge, Yarmouth, Dunwich, Ipswich and Colchester by the barons (Ramsay's *Angevin Empire*, 1903, *p*. 497). Bury St. Edmunds a stronghold of the king (Norgate, *John Lackland*, 1902, *pp*. 257-8). Louis himself fighting in the south of England. No evidence of Louis or his hordes ever being at Bury.
1216	Oct. 19. Death of John at Newark. Henry III succeeds to the throne.
1220	(*circa*). Richard of Newport, sacrist, destroys the old chapter-house and rebuilds it from foundations.
1220	Death of Herbert the prior. Richard of Insula (afterwards 12th abbot) succeeds him.
1224	Abbot Hugh at the Royal camp before Bedford Castle, attended by knights holding manors under St. Edmund.
1225	(*circa*). Abbot's Bridge built.
1229	Abbot Hugh II made Bishop of Ely: died August, 1254. Described by Matthew Paris as "flos nigrorum monachorum."
1229	Nov. 20. Richard of Insula recalled from Burton and installed as 12th abbot on St. Edmund's Day.

p. 247.

| 1234 | Abbot Richard sent abroad on an appeal to Pope Gregory IX. Attacked on his return with mortal illness, and dies at Pontigny. Buried in the chapter-house at Bury, where his skeleton was discovered on January 1, 1903, with skull sawn through and sternum severed (evidently for embalming purposes). | p. 247. |

1235   Henry of Rushbrook, prior of Bury, elected 13th abbot.

1235   Royal Charters granted to Abbot Henry to hold two fairs at Bury and a market at his manor of Melford.

1245   Abbot Henry excused by the Pope, on account of the gout, from attending the Council of Lyons.

1245   At the request of the convent, Henry III calls his newly-born son Edmund (founder of the house of Lancaster). Text of Royal letter in Arnold III. 28.

1248   July 5. Bull of Pope Innocent III (signed at Lyons) prescribing the solemn celebration of the feast of the translation of St. Edmund (April 29). Text in *Nov. Leg. Angl.* (1901) II. 574.

1248   Death of Abbot Henry: buried in chapter-house. Edmund of Walpole, LL.D., appointed 14th abbot.

1250   Henry III takes the Cross: the abbot does the same, exposing himself to general derision (Matt. Par. v. 110).

1252   Simon of Luton (afterwards abbot) made prior.

1254   Richard of Clare, seventh Earl of Gloucester, claims St. Edmund's manor of Mildenhall: threatened with excommunication by the Pope.

1254	Aug. Death of Hugh, Bishop of Ely (Abbot of Bury, 1213-29).
1256	Aug. Statutes approved by Pope Alexander IV for the governance of the Abbey of Bury, providing *inter alia* for "two persons watching the body of St. Edmund and two the church treasure and clock night and day."
1256	Dec. 31. Abbot Edmund died: buried in the chapter-house.
1257	Jan. 15. Simon of Luton, prior, elected 15th abbot: cost of confirmation by the Pope, 2,000 marks.
1263	Nov. Franciscan friars expelled from Bury, under a rescript from Pope Urban IV, and compelled to migrate to Babwell.
1264	(Easter). Serious conflict between the monastery and the burgesses. The abbot complains to the king: fine inflicted on the burgesses.
1265	Defeat and death of Simon de Montfort. Many barons of his party take shelter at Bury, but subsequently dislodged.
1267	February. Henry III summons the barons who owe military service to the Crown to meet him at Bury.
1272	Sept. 1. Henry III at Bury on his way to Norwich.
1272	Nov. 16. Death of Henry III (Rishanger says at Bury).
1275	April 17. Edward I and his Queen come to St. Edmundsbury on a pilgrimage, "as they had vowed in the Holy Land."
1275	July 1. Foundation stone of new Lady Chapel laid by Prior Robert.

p. <u>247</u>.

1279	April. Death of Abbot Simon at Melford: buried in the Lady Chapel, which he had built "at the cost of himself, his parents and his friends" (Leland, iv. 164).
1279	Dec. 28. John of Northwold, guest master of the abbey, solemnly received in the Abbey Church as 16th abbot, after having gone to Rome to be blessed by Pope Nicholas III. Cost of his journey, 1,175 marks, his credit from abbey being only 500 marks.
1281	A new division between the property of the abbot and that of the convent, sanctioned by Edward I in consideration of £1,000.
1285	Feb. 20. The King with the Queen and her three daughters make a pilgrimage to Bury.
1292	April 28. The King, with his son and daughters, again at Bury, remaining either at the abbey or the manor of Culford for ten days. Granted charter that none of his justices should sit within the banlieue of St. Edmund.
1292	Dispute between monastery and town. Royal Commission of inquiry sent down. The burgesses to present annually an alderman for confirmation by the abbot: the alderman to present four persons to the sacrist as keepers of the four gates.
1294	Mar. 18. Edward I again at St. Edmundsbury "with great devotion."
1296	Nov. Edward I holds a Parliament at Bury to obtain an aid from the clergy and people. Difficulties in its collection.
1301	Oct. 29. Death of Abbot John I: buried in the church before the choir altar.
1301	Nov. 30. Edward's I's letter giving permission for a new election.

1302	Jan. 2. Election of Thomas of Tottington (Samson's birthplace) as 17th abbot.
1305	Further disputes between the convent and the town. The king's justices impose fines on the aldermen and burgesses.
1312	Jan. 7. Death of Abbot Thomas: buried in north aisle of abbey church (part of his memorial brass now at Hedgerley church, Bucks). Succeeded by Richard of Draughton.
1326	Edward II spends Christmas at Bury.
1327	Great riots at Bury: the abbey plundered. The abbot seized and carried off, and eventually deported to Diest in Brabant. The outlying manors ravaged, and nearly the whole of the conventual and domestic buildings burnt: loss of property assessed at £140,000. Charter extorted by the townsmen from the convent. (French text in Arnold III. 302-317.)
1330	Sept. 13. Charter of Edward III granting free warren in all demesnes of the Abbey of St. Edmund, and a weekly market at Melford, with an annual fair of nine days.
1335	Death of Abbot Richard: buried in north aisle of the church. The sub-prior, William of Bernham, hastily elected 19th abbot for fear of the Pope's interference.
1345	Jan. 24. Completion of Richard of Bury's *Philobiblon*.
1345	Quarrel between the abbey and Bishop Bateman of Norwich. Morality and discipline of the abbey reported bad by diocesan commissioners.
1346	The abbot appeals to the Pope, and also sues Bishop Bateman in the King's Court, pleading the Charter of Hardicanute (1035): the judges give sentence in the abbot's favour.

1346	(*circa*). Completion of abbey gateway, erected after destruction of a previous gateway by the townspeople in the riots of 1327.
1351	Presentation to the abbot of three names for selection of an alderman to have charge of the municipal government of Bury. Admission by the abbot of John Ewell as a matter of favour.
1361	Death of Abbot William: buried in Lady Chapel. Henry of Hunstanton elected his successor, and proceeds to Avignon, but dies of the pestilence near that city before obtaining confirmation by the Pope.
1361	John of Brinkley appointed as 20th abbot by Pope Innocent VI.
1375	Date of last miracle recorded in Bodleian MS. 240 (Symon Broun, nearly lost at sea, vows to St. Edmund and is saved. *Nov. Leg. Anglie* (1901) vol. II. *p.* 678).
1379	Death of John of Brinkley at Elmswell: buried in the Lady Chapel. John of Timworth, sub-prior, elected by the monks 21st abbot. Urban VI appoints Edmund de Bromfeld instead, and a controversy ensues, lasting five years.
1381	Rebellion in East Anglia under Jack Strawe. Murder of John de Cambridge, the prior, and Sir John Cavendish, the chief justice. Town of Bury outlawed and fined 2,000 marks.
1383	Richard II and Anne of Bohemia visit Bury and remain ten days at the monastery, at an expense of 800 marks.
1384	June 4. Matters having at length been arranged with the Pope, John of Timworth's election as abbot is confirmed (died 1389).
1390	William of Cratfield elected 22nd abbot.

1400	Oct. 1. Thomas of Arundel, Archbishop of Canterbury, visits Bury: received as a visitor with much respect, but without a procession.	
1408	Nov. 25. Letters patent of King Henry IV finally deciding, in favour of Bury Abbey, the disputed question as to the jurisdiction of the Liberty of St. Edmund over Hadleigh and Eleigh.	*pp.* 76-8, 239.
1410	Catalogue of 195 Monastic Libraries (including that of Bury), compiled by John Boston, monk of Bury.	
1415	June 18. Death of Cratfield. William of Exeter elected 23rd abbot.	
1424	William Exeter causes the marble tomb of Ording (and (?) of Samson) in the chapter-house to be renewed.	*p.* 247.
1424-33	Building of the present St. Mary's Church on the site of an older church in S.W. corner of the cemetery of the abbey.	
1427	Thomas Beaufort, second son of John of Gaunt, buried in Abbey Church (coffin discovered and re-interred 1772).	
1429	Death of William Exeter. William Curteys or Curtis elected 24th abbot.	
1430	Dec. 18. Fall of Southern side of western tower.	
1430	Dec. 30. Fall of Eastern side of western tower. Immediate steps taken to contract for a new tower.	
1430	Abbot Curteys builds a library for the abbey (see his regulations for use of books in *James, pp.* 109-11).	

1432	Ruins of tower cleared away. Rebuilding commenced: estimated cost, 60,000 ducats of gold.
1433-4	Visit of Henry VI to Bury Abbey from Christmas till St. George's Day. The monastery presents him with a magnificently illuminated *Life of St. Edmund*, by John Lydgate (now in Brit. Mus. Harl. MS. 2278).
1446	Sept. 17. Henry VI writes to Abbot Curteys to ask him to be present at laying of foundation stone of King's College, Cambridge, on Michaelmas Day.
1446	Death of Curteys. Succeeded by William Babington as 25th abbot.
1447	Feb. 10. Parliament at Bury, in the Abbey refectory. Duke Humphrey of Gloucester present, and arrested (Feb. 18) for high treason.
1447	Nov. 13. Charter of Henry VI confirming the abbey privileges. (Text in Arnold III. 357.)
1449	Royal Charter granted, freeing the Abbot of all aids to the King for forty marks a year.
1453	Death of Abbot Babington: John Boon, or Bohun, appointed 26th abbot.
1462	General pardon granted by Edward IV to the Abbot and monks, whose sympathies had been Lancastrian.
1462	Nov. 17. A lost Abbey register bought by John Broughton, and presented by him to the monastery at the instance of Abbot Boon.
1465	Jan. 20. Abbey Church completely gutted by fire. (St. Edmund's shrine said to have been saved.) Abbot Boon spends and collects large sums for its repair and rebuilding.

1469	Death of Abbot Boon: buried in the Lady Chapel. Succeeded by Robert of Ixworth as 27th abbot.
1474	Richard of Hengham appointed 27th abbot.
1479	Thomas of Rattlesden appointed 28th abbot.
1479	May. William of Worcester visits the Abbey and takes measurements of the various buildings.
1486	Visit of Henry VII to Bury.
1497	William of Codenham appointed 29th abbot.
1513	Death of Codenham. John Reeve of Melford appointed 30th and last abbot.
1532	Abbot Reeve assists at the funeral of Abbot Islip of Westminster.
1533	July 21. Mary Tudor, sister of Henry VIII, buried in great state at the Abbey (subsequently re-interred in St. Mary's Church).
1535	Nov. 5. Letter from John Ap Rice to Thomas Cromwell as to the state of morals and worship of relics at Bury Abbey and enclosing *compertes* of proceedings (*Compendium Compertorum* now at Record Office).
1536	Nov. 26. Grant by the Abbey to Thomas Cromwell and his son Gregory of an annuity of £10.
1538	(*circa*). Visit of Leland the antiquary to Bury, in search of ancient books and records.
1538	Sept. Sir John Williams, Richard Pollard, Philip Parys and John Smyth report to Cromwell that they have been to St.

Edmundsbury, "where we founde a riche shryne which was very comberous to deface. We have takyn in the said monastery in golde and sylver MMMMM marks and above, over and besydes a well and riche crosse with emereddes, as also dyvers and sundry stones of great value, and yet we have left the churche, abbott and convent very well ffurnesshed with plate of sylver necessary for the same" (MS. Cotton. Cleop. E. iv. 229). The actual amount of plate taken at 'His Majesty's visitation' on this occasion was 1,553 oz gold plate, 6,853 oz. gilt plate, 933 oz. parcel-gilt plate, 190 oz. white plate. (*Monastic Treasures*, 1836). See also under Dec. 2, 1539.

1539   Nov. 4. Deed of surrender of Bury Abbey signed by Abbot Reeve, Prior Thomas Denysse of Ryngstede and 41 other monks.

1539   Nov. 7. Sir Richard Rich, Sir A. Wingfield, Ric. Southwell, Wm. Petre, John Ap Rice, and T. Mildmay inform Henry VIII of the surrender of the Abbey: they "have taken the plate and best ornaments of the house" for the King, and have sold the rest. They also ask whether they are "to deface the church or other edifices of the house." The lead and the bells (if the house be defaced) will be worth 4,500 marks.

1539   Dec. 2. Indent of Richard Southwell of amount of plate taken from Bury Abbey—150 oz. gilt plate, 145 oz. parcel-gilt plate, and 2,162 oz. white plate, besides a pair of birrall candlesticks (handed to the King), and an ornamented mitre (*Monastic Treasures*, 1836). [Thus, with the spoils of 1538, 1,553 oz. gold plate (all on the first occasion), and 10,433 oz. silver plate, were taken from the Abbey.]

SECTION IV

FROM THE DISSOLUTION TO 1903

1540	March 30. Death of ex-Abbot Reeve; buried in the chancel of St. Mary's Church.
1550	The first of the thirty grammar schools founded by Edward VI established at Bury.
1560	Feb. 14. Site of Monastery sold by Queen Elizabeth for £412 19s. 4d. to John Eyer; by him transferred to Thomas Badby.
1578	Aug. 7. Queen Elizabeth at Bury.
1599	Over a hundred books from Bury Abbey in the hands of William Smart, a "Postman" of Ipswich. Given by him to Pembroke College, Cambridge.
1606	Apl. 3. Bury made a Borough by Charter of James I. (Borough Motto: *Sacrarium Regis, Cunabula Legis*).
1634	Condition of the site of the Abbey described by William Hawkins of Hadleigh in his "Corolla Varia."
1644	Publication at Toulouse of Caseneuve's "Vie de St. Edmond," alleging that the body of the saint was at the basilica of St. Sernin there, and had been brought over by Louis in 1216. Caseneuve describes, misquoting Matthew Paris (II. 663) the alleged pillage by Louis of "Toutes les églises du comté de Suffolk," refers to the fact that in those days "les Chrétiens faisaient gloire d'enlever par un devot larcin les reliques des saints," and says "Il est croyable que les Francais en firent autant de celles de St. Edmond" (*cf.* 1216, 1256, 1901).
1745	Publication at Oxford by Rev. Dr. Oliver Battely of *Antiquitates S. Edmundi Burgi ad annum MCCLXXII perductæ*, written by his uncle, Dr. John Battely (died 1708).

1761	Ancient gates of town pulled down by order of Corporation.
1772	Some excavations on site of Church, made by Mr. King, and reported in vol. III. of Archaeologia.
1805	Publication of *An Illustration of the Monastic History and Antiquities of the Town and Abbey of St. Edmund's Bury*, by Richard Yates, D.D., F.R.S. (1769-1834).
1806	Site of Abbey comes into the hands of the Hervey family, the present possessors.
1840	Rokewode's Edition of Latin text of *Chronicle of Jocelin of Brakelond*, published by Camden Soc.
1843	Carlyle's *Past and Present* published.
1843	Publication of second edition—including fragment of Part II projected in 1805—of Yates' History of Bury (Remainder of Yates' materials amongst Egerton MSS. in British Museum).
1844	T. E. Tomlins' English translation of *Jocelin's Chronicle*.
1850	S. Tymms' *Bury Wills* (Camd. Soc.).
1865	Papers by Mr. Gordon M. Hills on antiquities of Bury St. Edmunds in *Journal British Archæological Association*, vol. xxi. *pp.* 32-56 and 104-140.
1869	July 20. British Archæological Association at Bury: paper on Abbey read by Mr. Alfred W. Morant.
1890	Publication of J. R. Thompson's *Records of St. Edmund* [mostly based on Battely and the legendary chronicles].

1890	Publication of vol. I. of *Memorials of St. Edmund's Abbey* (Rolls series), edited by T. Arnold (vol. II. published 1892, vol. III. 1896).
1893	Publication of *St. Edmund King and Martyr*, by Rev. Father Mackinlay, O.S.B. [picturesque and interesting, but uncritical].
1895	Publication of Dr. Montague R. James' two papers on (1) the Library (2) the Church of "The Abbey of St. Edmund at Bury" (Camb. Antiq. Soc., 8vo. Publications No. xxviii.).
1901	Publication of *Nova Legenda Anglie* (Ox. Univ. Press), containing in vol. II. the full "Vita et passio cum miraculis sancti Edmundi," compiled at Bury in the 14th Century (Bodl. MS. 240).
1901	July 25. Landing at Newhaven, for the new Roman Catholic Cathedral of Westminster, of bones from Toulouse said to be those of St. Edmund (*cf.* 1216, 1256, 1644.).
1901	Sept. 5. Letter in *The Times* showing cause against these bones being those of St. Edmund.
1901	Sept. 9. Cardinal Vaughan admits at Newcastle-on-Tyne that, in view of facts stated, "the relics are not genuine."
1902	Publication of Lord Francis Hervey's *Suffolk in the XVIIth Century*, containing in Appendix a critical study of the legends about St. Edmund's life and martyrdom.

3

1902-	(Winter). Excavations on site of chapter-house.
1903	Jan. 1. Discovery on the site of the chapter-house of five stone coffins with skeletons, in the positions assigned in a Bury MS. of circa 1425 (now at Douai) to the burial places of Abbots Ording (1146-56), SAMSON (1182-

pp. 225, 247.

1211), Richard of Insula (1229-34), Henry of Rushbrook (1234-46), and Edmund of Walpole (1248-56). A sixth skeleton (uncoffined) also found in a line with these coffins to the west—doubtless that of Abbot Hugh I (1156-80).

CPSIA information can be obtained
at www.ICGtesting.com
Printed in the USA
LVHW041952061121
702610LV00006B/311